Contents

MW00682819

Dedication

This book is offered with love to every child welfare worker whose life has been dedicated to helping children and youth. You make a difference!

It is also dedicated to my daughter, Susan Sharp, and her husband, Justin Mirgeaux. Your support is cherished.

Finally, I would like to dedicate this book to my husband, Philip Diaz, who has been my greatest advocate. Thank you for sharing your editorial skills, insights, and time. You are a wonderful life companion.

Acknowledgments

This book would not have gotten off the ground had it not been for the support of the publishing staff at the Child Welfare League of America. Peggy Tierney was immediately behind the project, backed up by Eve Klein and Sue Brite. My editor, Julie Gwin, was encouraging and insightful. President/CEO Shay Bilchek was, as always, open and approachable.

A project such as this brings into focus how many wonderful people are ready and willing to make a contribution. I wish to thank the young people who agreed to spend time answering my questions. Your courage and resilience shined through. I would also like to thank the more than 100 child welfare workers who kindly volunteered to answer my survey. You represent different regions, yet share a wonderful dedication to our kids.

I would also like to thank the child welfare administrators who spoke frankly with me about the challenges they are facing in this new century. They include Betty S. Carley, David Bundy, Diane DeMark, James Patrick, Krista Goldstine-Cole, Patricia O'Gorman, Carol Brown, Doug Vaughn, Jill Kinney, Nancy P. Gannon, Jim Clark, William A. Shetler, Philip Diaz, Marie Sophie, Greg Britton, and Shay Bilchek.

A genteel thank you to Antonio DeNicholas, PhD, for contributing his philosophical input and beautiful poem translation.

A special thank you to Alvin Lynard Killough, PhD. His expertise on the cultural diversity chapter was informative and powerful.

Charlotte McCullogh was extraordinarily helpful in setting the record straight about current funding initiatives and trends, not to mention other aspects of child welfare work.

Gracious thanks to Maria Colavito, PhD, for her patient description of biocultures as well as her support. Her enthusiasm is contagious.

Thanks to Sandy Brookshire and Eneida Gomez, MD, for their input.

And to Louise McLaughlin, who pulled the technical material together so that I could deliver the book in one piece.

Paree Stivers, PsyD, spent hours going over chapters and providing valuable editorial comments. She doggedly followed this book from its inception through to its end. Thank you for such clear and practical advice. Your integrity and commitment to children is profound, and I am blessed to know you.

There are no better teachers then our own children. I want to thank my daughter, Susan Sharp, and her husband, Justin Mirgeaux, for being such excellent role models and great friends.

Finally, I would like to thank my husband, Phil Diaz, for reading and rereading the book. His remarks kept me on track and reminded me why I set out to write it in the first place.

Introduction

I did not want this book to read like a conventional textbook. Beneath a diligence to get the facts straight, my intention was to write an informative, supportive guide that leads readers toward a deeper understanding of child welfare work, as well as greater personal awareness.

The 21st century represents a new era for child advocates, because it is challenging conventional child and family intervention strategies. In recent years, rates of violence, drug use, and mental health problems in children have grown rapidly. These conditions contribute to a more ambiguous and dangerous work experience for child welfare workers. Consequently, I also wanted this book to offer relevant information and practical advice. I hope you will find it a helpful guide.

Two themes emerged as I began to write. The first section, "21st-Century Challenges," focuses on child welfare issues. Child welfare workers need to stay current, so these chapters include an overview of the 21st-century child welfare system, new and complementary neural research, and social, physical, and mental health problems in high-risk children and youth. Also included are handy references, such as lists of drugs often abused by children and youth as well as pediatric psychiatric medications.

Part II, "21st-Century Strategies," addresses central work issues, such as worker accountability, cultural competence, problems on the job, worker burnout, and worker resilience. Finally, Chapter 10 discusses why people are called to child welfare service.

Writing this book has been a wonderful experience. I have had the opportunity to interview front-line workers, foster parents, supervisors, administrators, and researchers. They all share a strong commitment to our children. The young people I interviewed were articulate and honest. Their stories were powerful, and I was honored to be in their company.

Comments made by child welfare workers and administrators are scattered throughout the book. Most of these quotes come from interviews as well as surveys completed by more than 100 child welfare workers.

As a die-hard child advocate, I have become frustrated over the years because child welfare work has not received the recognition it deserves. Every day, thousands of dedicated men and women guide and protect high-risk kids. Yet our profession seems to remain a "stepchild" in the collective public consciousness. We still receive lesser pay and strong criticism. I hope this book will help increase the public's appreciation.

The bottom line is that child welfare continues to be in crisis. Only a monumental effort from legislators, human service administrators, and enlightened citizens can change this fact. Perhaps the 21st century will usher in better times for child welfare as others share ownership of our nation's children.

—*Kathryn Brohl*

PART I

21st-Century Challenges

Bad times have a scientific value....We learn geology the
morning after the earthquake.
—*Ralph Waldo Emerson*

CHAPTER 1

Six 21st-Century Child Welfare Work Challenges

Just When I Knew What I Was Doing,
They Changed the Rules!

A Child Welfare Worker's Story

I have been doing this work for more than 30 years. My first job was directing youth activities at our local YMCA after graduating from college. But I grew bored and wanted to take my interest in child advocacy to a different level. So I decided to go for my graduate degree in social work.

Graduate school was great. There was a good deal of support for small group experience and discussion. Our professors were pretty interesting. Unfortunately, many of them never spent much time out in the field, and I had some catching up to do after graduation.

I worked with kids whose families had lived in rural Kentucky, West Virginia, and Tennessee, but who later moved to our city looking for jobs. I didn't know much about their culture. But I learned...often, the hard way.

Back then, kids in that particular state were placed in juvenile detention because they missed school or ran away from home. Little was known about sexual abuse, and I recall overhearing police officers talk about how an 8- or 9-year-old had "seduced" her daddy. Their comments drove me crazy.

Sexual abuse against children still happens, and other problems that worry child welfare workers have gotten worse. Youngsters now use guns to express their anger, and others have lost their parents to substance abuse. Children are getting involved in drugs or alcohol at younger ages, and more live with only one parent. There are so many things distracting kids. Violence is every- where. Even the Internet is becoming dangerous.

Other things have changed since I began working in child welfare, as well. Paperwork was simpler. Units of service were unheard of. We went to work and got paid. Sure, we had to record what we did, but it's nothing like today.

When I started, time was set aside for supervision. Even graduate school was underwritten by our agency. We were very excited by family-, reality-, and client-centered thera- pies. There were opportunities to put theoretical training to practice, because we had the support of our supervi- sors. And agencies seemed to understand the value of investing in training.

About 10 years into my career, I moved to another state and, from a professional perspective, immediately noticed a big difference. There was no state tax to support child welfare. Consequently, staff training was not a priority. There was no money. The state child protective service agency at times hired people with marginal backgrounds, and employees sometimes became supervisors simply because they had the time in, not because they did better work.

I've had different job titles over the years, and I've seen a lot of child welfare workers come and go. Some of the good ones leave for various reasons. They need to make more money or they become discouraged. And over time the work can be exhausting.

Politicians say the same things now that they said 30 years ago. But let's face it, children don't vote. And insurance companies have just gotten mean. How can they rationalize putting a child back at home so soon after a suicide attempt? How is it possible to heal 10 years of hell in 5 days?

I'm glad so many inroads have been made with regard to understanding the brain, because now we know why kids behave the way they do after their traumatic experiences. And there is public awareness about rape and domestic violence. But I'm sad that new workers may never have the opportunities we had. They may not have an inspiring supervisor or they think that HMOs have always been around.

Would I choose this work again? I think so, because I still believe that one person can make a difference in a child's life. But I feel like I was given a good start. I wish my young colleagues had the same opportunities.

Changes in Child Welfare Work

The one certainty in life is change. In the past few decades, changes in the child welfare system have been dizzying. Varied funding streams, new research findings, extreme levels of paperwork, and heightened substance abuse in parents are some of the challenges confronting workers. Every day, more than 7,700 kids in the United States are reported abused or neglected, and for those who advocate in their behalf, follow-up investigations and interventions are becoming more ambiguous and dangerous.

For example, children and family members can be unpredictable, depending on their sobriety level or mental health status. Case responsibility can get confused, or a caregiver can decide she does not need her antipsychotic medication. Funding can be cut and monies diverted because of inclement political weather. Children may suddenly demonstrate bizarre behaviors or be coerced by family members to recant their abuse disclosures.

We sometimes ask ourselves, "How did I get here?", and the answer usually relates to our childhood. People who become child welfare workers often demonstrate their ability to do meaningful work long before they earn their first paychecks. They report that the urge to help seems natural and can even give meaning to their personal suffering. Consequently, planning for a career in child welfare becomes an extension of their personalities.

But although we are naturally drawn toward this work, we are usually clueless about how difficult it can be. The old adage "ignorance is bliss" applies to many. Few vocations require as much emotional energy, flexibility, patience, and kind detachment.

For instance, people working in "regular jobs" don't stay awake nights, wondering if a decision they have made means the difference between giving renewed meaning to a child's life or exposing him or her to additional danger. Child protection workers deeply fear the death of one of their children. And the truth is, it happens. But the public perceives that a 100% reduction in child deaths is realistic now, even when the child protection system is underfunded and workers are overwhelmed.

If a child in protective custody dies, politicians often assume an "off with their heads" posture. Workers are not infallible, which is difficult for the public to accept. The public expects workers to be clairvoyant. The decisions placed before child welfare workers are tough and not getting easier.

Most people recognize that child welfare work was different before our society became more drug dependent and violent. In 1962, E. R. Braithwaite, a child worker and author of *To Sir with Love*, wrote another book, *Paid Servant*. It describes his story of struggling to place a 4-year-old named Ronnie in foster care. Braithwaite encountered the predictable players from the world of child welfare—a mother who sold her body, a biased welfare system, and a troubled child. As a person of color, Braithwaite described a frustrating journey. It was all he could do to awaken his colleagues' interest, let alone compassion. Yet, he was able to travel easily around his city and experienced relatively few physical threats. At the end of the story, Braithwaite waved goodbye to Ronnie and his new foster family, while mildly lamenting that the child forgot to give him a hug.

In contrast, another worker's account was published 30 years later. *Turning Stones: A Caseworker's Story* (Parent, 1996) also describes an author's work with neglected and abused children. But in 1996, Parent's clients were heroin or cocaine addicted. His heavy caseload prohibited time

---

Child Abuse and Neglect Definitions

Emotional Maltreatment—Parental or other caregiver acts or omissions, such as rejecting, terrorizing, berating, ignoring, or isolating a child, that cause, or are likely to cause, serious impairment of their physical, social, mental, or emotional capacities of the child.

Neglect—Failure of parents or other caregivers, for reasons not solely due to poverty, to provide the child with needed age-appropriate care, including food, clothing, shelter, protection from harm, supervision appropriate to the child's development, hygiene, education, and medical care.

Physical Abuse—Physical acts by parents or caregivers that cause, or could have caused, physical injury in a child.

Sexual Abuse—Sexual activity by a parent or other caregiver with a child including, but not limited to, any kind of sexual contact through persuasion, physical force, or other coercive means; exploitation through sexual activity that is allowed, encouraged, or coerced; and child prostitution or pornography. (Child Welfare League of America, 1999, pp. 192–194)

Child protective services (CPS) usually intervene in allegations of child abuse or neglect by parents or other caregivers. Law enforcement handles allegations of criminal acts against children by adults or juveniles. A few states, however, are considering using law enforcement to take the lead with regard to following up on allegations of child abuse neglect by parents or other caregivers.

---

with his young clients, and he was overwhelmed with paperwork. The death of a child he was supervising contributed to his decision to leave his profession.

Six 21st-Century Challenges

Advocating for children in this century requires that workers need to consider some pretty intense challenges if they want to do a good job. For example, accountability is now more narrowly defined. Workers must jump through higher hoops related to child welfare laws and procedures, as our society has become more litigious.

Child welfare workers also need to understand funding sources and properly document their work so they get paid. In addition, health and social issues in children and youth have taken a disturbing turn with the rise in gun availability and violence. Consequently, workers need to know how to identify children's problems early so that they do not have to deal with more severe physical and psychological conditions later (for related definitions, see next page).

Neuroscience is expanding awareness of the environment's power over healthy growth and development in children. It is necessary that workers comprehend new research relevant to the causes behind child and youth problems. They must also assert themselves to receive adequate direct and indirect compensation. Finally, workers must consciously avoid becoming burned out.

Challenge One—Accountability
Defining and Measuring Success

Defining Success. Defining success in child welfare is elusive, and the national mandate of "leave no child behind" is not hitting home when it comes to identifying specific success outcomes with children and families. For example, is success measured by fewer child abuse and neglect reports? Or is it measured only by the number of children under CPS's supervision? And how is success monitored, tested, and duplicated? National, state, and local agencies need to reach consensus in defining *success* in child welfare.

Data-Driven Assessments. Assessing our work has undergone a transformation. According to James E. Patrick, chief operating officer of one the country's largest child welfare agencies, accountability in child welfare is moving from focusing on process to outcome. Child welfare is becoming data or performance driven.

Outcomes are now based on measuring client improvement in a variety of ways, including quality assessment. Agencies place greater emphasis on measuring how well the job was done with clients. In the past, a worker may have assigned a child a mental health counselor, but his or her treatment may have been loosely defined and open ended. This process approach did not challenge conventional treatment paradigms and created a rather generalized and ambiguous approach to helping children. Data-driven assessments are more specific to improvement goals and timelines.

A successful transition from process- to outcome-centered accountability depends largely on measurements that mirror current research and common sense.

Security-Compliant Technical Systems. Security-compliant technical systems that support child welfare accountability have been historically behind other professions. For the most part, child welfare workers' collection and collation of data has been poor compared with banks and hospitals, which place greater emphasis on training staff on using computers and providing up-to-date equipment. Child welfare is continually challenged to keep pace. Perhaps underwriting technical support is difficult to sell to funding sources, because the sources are already stretched thin and technical support has not been given priority with other child safety considerations.

Family Preservation Versus Family Safety

Another accountability issue centers on family preservation versus child safety through out-of-home placement. Child welfare administrators are looking for answers to two questions. Is it safer for kids to remain at home and use support services? Or are kids best helped by being placed outside the home, while everyone works with support services toward family reunification?

Some states that had emphasized the family preservation approach to child welfare dramatically reverted to the child safety approach when children died. Maintaining a balance between family preservation and child safety is an ongoing accountability issue for child welfare workers. Unfortunately, these policies can suddenly get revamped during an election year.

Filling Staff Positions to Meet Stricter Timelines

Accountability has become further refined through stricter timelines pertaining to child abuse investigation and family reunification. These timelines vary from state to state and are necessary, but can sometimes breed sloppy work when understaffed agencies have too many cases to handle.

In addition, the Adoption and Safe Families Act of 1997 requires that family reunification must occur for children placed in foster or residential care within 12 months. Its intention is to keep kids from languishing in out-of-home placement for long periods and to achieve permanency for them in a timely manner. If this does not happen, the government terminates parental custody. The law, although a step in the right direction, can put workers under pressure to set timelines that can be difficult for some types of clients, such as substance abusers, to follow.

Federal and state accountability requirements are much easier to complete when agencies have sufficient staff. In many parts of the country, however, hiring and keeping child welfare workers and foster parents is a problem. According to Jill Kinney, Director of Home Safe in Seattle, a national "natural helper" training center, "Some organizations have as much as 50%-80% turnover, while others cannot fill the slots they have." Saundra, a child welfare professional who works in the Outer Banks of North Carolina, remarked, "There are not enough qualified people to fill the positions now; what will happen in 10 years?" Finding staff to meet these needs is one of the toughest challenges in the new millennium.

Client Collaboration

Years ago, accountability focused more responsibility on clients, not agencies. But things are changing. An Ohio child welfare veteran said, "Three decades ago, people in power, such as politicians, generally demonstrated more confidence in the child welfare system. We were not put under a magnifying glass when problems occurred. Now, there are finer checks and balances." She believes that child welfare is moving toward becoming a service industry, creating a shift in the way social workers have related to their clients.

For example, empowering clients, a critical issue in strengthening families, is now viewed as a collaborative effort by innovators in the field. Agencies are asking case managers to give greater consideration to the opinions of birthfamilies and adoptive families. In many states, foster parents are taking a more active role in the decisionmaking process about their foster children, closing the gap in the child welfare hierarchy.

Along this same theme, self-directed care is a newer approach to helping families. Theoretically, clients are able to use support services with the help of a life coach as they work together on care plans. In this type of system, the assistance money follows the client.

Cultural Competence

Understanding different cultures and nontraditional family structures is a bigger part of child welfare work today than it was in the past. Workers must be sensitive to family diversity, including same-sex relationships.

Child welfare workers are also learning that they can build better relations among immigrant and ethnic populations when language and ethnicity are understood and respected. This is easier said than done, because many child welfare workers have not been familiarized with Creole, Vietnamese, Serbian, Chinese, or Korean families before they begin working with these populations.

The 21st century is introducing biology culture as another diversity consideration. Evidence is emerging to substantiate that we demonstrate our uniqueness because of our early brain patterning or habituation. Discussion is sure to continue around neural science's contribution to understanding diversity.

Demonstrating Affection

Child welfare workers have become wary about demonstrations of affection with children. As an outgrowth of the number of sexual abuse allegations in child care and residential treatment in the late 1980s and early 1990s, workers have become keenly aware about how they demonstrate caring.

Reprehensible acts performed by the small minority of former employees, as well as poor investigative work, affected many workers. "I am extremely careful around our young female residents, to the extent I won't even give them a pat on the back," said one male recreation technician. "It's too risky." Although workers must always maintain awareness about natural fears and anxieties exhibited in abused children, many workers withhold well-intentioned physical demonstrations of caring that are necessary for healthy child development. Tighter accountability guidelines can sometimes create self-consciousness in helpers, as well as a lack of spontaneity in demonstrating care.

Professional Development

Professional development has improved in various ways. More child care workers and foster parents are completing required accreditation programs. Trainers are instructing investigators in more effective ways to complete nonbiased investigations. Peer mentoring is becoming a trend in helping workers feel more support. Cross-training among agencies help workers understand and use wraparound services for clients is growing, and

Child Welfare Funding Is Excessively Stressed

The current system of child welfare funding is excessively stressed. Although the trend is moving toward financial justification and time limitations, child welfare cannot always function well within those constraints. Child welfare has very little power over front-end investigations and back-end court recommendations. Workers cannot discharge or refuse supervision to young clients and their families, and no maximum medical improvement exists when it comes to their well-being.

agency administrators are working at other ways of minimizing staff isolation. Despite this, continuing education and training related to best practices is not keeping up with staff need.

Challenge Two—Funding and Documentation

Funding has always been one of the biggest challenges in child welfare. Experts agree that many states are unable to consider upgrading their current systems of care without receiving additional funds.

Documentation has changed dramatically in the past 10 years with regard to being paid. Identifying and recording units of service was not something front-line workers had to think about in the past, but it is now a daily consideration. The following are some other funding trends.

Community-Based Care and Privatization

A growing interest has emerged around the issue of community-based care, such as county oversight of child safety. For example, in the area of child abuse and neglect, local sheriff's departments may contract with the state to do investigative work, while community nonprofits may contract to follow up with case management and aftercare for children who become temporary or permanent wards of the state.

Privatization moves total management of funds, services, and monitoring to for-profit or nonprofit contractees. These agencies essentially control a child welfare system. This is similar to health maintenance organizations (HMOs).

Not All Caregivers Receive Financial Assistance

It is estimated that a quarter of all the nation's welfare cases involve caregivers who are relatives and collect welfare benefits themselves or in behalf of the children. But in the majority of households where children are living with relatives, the family is not receiving public assistance. Some relatives do not want the stigma, some are unaware that they are eligible, and others have been wrongly denied.

Many states are already following community-based care models because child welfare is county- or city-run. Other states transitioning from state-run child protection are now choosing between privatization and community-based care methodologies.

Documenting Services

Funding is now separated into different categories, or silos, such as mental health, juvenile justice, substance abuse, education, child welfare, and domestic violence. The separated dollars are paid per units of documented service. Units of service are authorized for each type of care, and some have been reduced to 15 minutes in length. Consequently, workers are accounting for every 15 minutes of their workday.

Furthermore, each type of intervention has different intervention criteria that must be documented. The documentation has led to volumes of additional paperwork. Most child welfare workers feel demoralized by spending so much time away from direct service, because documentation overemphasizes the least rewarding part of their job. Workers report that documentation takes more than one-quarter of their time.

When one worker was asked about the number of hours a week she spent on paperwork, she replied, "Too much!" Another man responded, "There's got to be a better way! I spend so much time filling out forms to justify my work, when I could be building relationships with my clients. What happened to checking the boxes?" One administrator expressed surprise when hearing that workers spend one-fourth of their time away from direct service. He said, "Quite frankly, under the current circumstances, I would think it's at least one-third of employee time."

Integrating Services

To keep costs under control and to avoid service duplication, some states are experimenting with integrating funding silos and blending services. According to Charlotte McCullough, a national child welfare consultant, "Ten years down the road, we may see states speaking more in terms of integrated services. Up to now, what predicts a child's intervention depends largely on what service door she comes through. Integration is preferable over fragmented services driven by categorical funding streams."

Because funding is tied to specific services, it is not unusual for workers to spend a lot of time trying to link clients to the right service. For example, a single parent on disability might qualify for different services than a substance-abusing parent. This places a strain on parents who have been assigned multiple tasks, such as completing classes and obtaining economic independence under strict timelines. These situations can further pressure child welfare workers. It is hoped that integrating services will make the work easier.

HMOs and Medicaid

The introduction of HMOs and changes in Medicaid have increased worker responsibilities, as they attempt to accommodate insurance guidelines, advocate for their clients, and fill out paperwork. Payment for services often requires preauthorization by the insurance carrier to begin a specific intervention, such as substance abuse counseling. To cap their costs, HMOs are making their criteria more restrictive. According to Diane DeMark, an expert in funding development, "If minute criteria is not followed exactly as requested, providers don't get paid. And the burden of proof always rests with them."

A frightening picture is emerging. For example, Medicaid is obligated to provide services for anyone eligible to receive them. But Medicaid's funds are capped, and funding allotments in most states have not kept up with current need. Consequently, the criteria bar is raised higher and higher to keep costs down. Many agencies have had to stop providing outpatient services because they could not meet the criteria and afford to pay licensed therapists, liability insurance, and other overhead costs associated with Medicaid reimbursement.

HMOs also contract to administer services, but they get paid to save their contractors' money. If they do not, they risk losing service contracts. Consumers are stuck in the middle, as HMOs try to please their contractors while looking after the needs of their patients.

As part of their goal to save money, insurance companies are mandating shorter timelines for treatment. James D. Clark, CEO of Daniel, Inc., the oldest child care agency in Florida, tells this story about the changes in private insurance funding:

> Eight years ago, our agency was 1 out of 100 residential treatment providers for an established insurance company. Five years ago, we were 1 out of 3. Three years ago, we withdrew our agency because the HMO would not pay for disturbed children to stay in our facility longer than two weeks, even though treatment experts recommend several months for conduct-disordered kids.

Brief therapy is a popular treatment theory often recommended by funding sources, but it pressures staff to get the job done before basic steps can be taken to help children feel safe with their treatment team, let alone address their mental health conditions.

Other Funding Avenues

To address funding, states are considering other creative avenues. Some states are considering using incentives, such as bonuses, if contracting agencies are able to operate within budget. They are also considering penalizing contractors if outcome goals have not been reached.

Some communities are considering levying special children's taxes to finance child welfare initiatives. Although it is never popular to ask taxpayers for money, in the long run, it may cost less. Ultimately, child welfare supervision is compromised when agencies are ever-mindful of the bottom line. Managers find that orienting staff toward financial justification can take time away from training on new practices and direct supervision.

Welfare to Work and Temporary Assistance to Needy Families (TANF) Implementation

As a result of the government's incentive to save taxpayers money, it enacted the 1996 Welfare to Work law. The law has affected children, especially black children in urban areas. A recent study indicated that more children are living with neither parent as a result of the pressures placed on parents to work and maintain homes while earning low wages. The University of California and the Rand Corporation analyzed the effect of welfare changes on children's living arrangements and found a very strong link between welfare reform and the number of children living with relatives other than parents. On average, they found that the share of black children living in cities without parents more than doubled after the changes. Researchers calculated about 200,000 more black urban children now live without a parent.

Not to minimize the effect on children, Barbara Ehrenreich (2001) joined the ranks of $6- and $7-an-hour workers and chronicled her experience in the book, *Nickel and Dimed: On (Not) Getting by in America*. She worked the same jobs as parents in Florida, Maine, and Minnesota who were struggling to support themselves and their children on poverty-level wages. Erhrenreich discovered that the work was hard and she needed two jobs to live indoors. For many people working for minimum wage, cars are luxuries and health insurance is fleeting. Consequently, more children are living with extended family members.

As families maximize TANF funds, children will likely be affected. Fallout could include a rise in neglect and abuse as a result of the stress experienced by parents struggling to make ends meet. The Welfare to Work initiative could also potentially create a rise in the number of homeless families.

Challenge Three—Child and Youth Social and Health Issues

The Good News

The news about child and youth issues is good and bad. Improvement exists in some areas. The Office of Juvenile Justice and Delinquency Prevention (OJJDP) reports that America's youth are committing fewer crimes. For instance, the U.S. Census Bureau's National Crime Victimization Survey found that, in 1998, youth crime was at its lowest rate in the 25-year history of that survey. According to the survey, "In almost every crime category, except the notable exception of gun crime, today's youth are much better behaved." This means that fewer kids are burglarizing houses or stealing cars. It does not mean that they have acquired better manners.

The Annie E. Casey Foundation's annual KIDS COUNT report states that between 1990 and 1998, infant mortality fell 22% and deaths of children ages 1 to 14 fell 23%. Other statistics include births to teenagers falling 19% and the high school drop-out rate declining 10% (Meckler, 2001). Although additional reasons exist for this positive information, it points to the fact that child welfare professionals have been doing their jobs.

All 50 states now offer low-cost or free health care insurance for children who qualify. Most uninsured children are eligible even if their parents work. Eligibility varies from state to state, but some families earning up to $36,000 a year may qualify for programs that cover doctor visits, immunizations, hospitalizations, and more. Unfortunately, approximately 5 million eligible children are not receiving these benefits. One of the reasons is the stigma attached to welfare benefits when parents work. In other words, parental pride is a factor. Another reason is that caregivers report feeling intimidated by the paperwork.

The Not-So-Good News

In spite of the good news, things have not gotten better for kids when it comes to their mental health and substance abuse conditions. According to Levy and Orlans (1998), more children are not developing secure attachments to protective caregivers—the most important factor in successful child development. They stated that in their estimation, approximately 800,000 children with severe attachment disorder are brought to the attention of the child welfare system each year. These kids have conduct disorders with severe levels of maladjustment. This can stress workers who are already challenged by inadequate funding, fewer resources, and stringent accountability.

Many children in the child welfare system suffer from biochemical-related mental health problems, such as fetal alcohol syndrome and other conditions that occur as a result of prenatal exposure to drugs. Greater numbers of children are also suffering from health problems such as obesity, asthma, and the early onset of diabetes II. Life-threatening sexually transmitted diseases, such as AIDS and hepatitis B and C, are health maintenance sentences for children and youth as well. Long-term planning for these children can conflict with short-term planning guidelines and fickle funding streams.

Mental Illness

Mental illness in children continues to be underdiagnosed. Nancy Gannon, Deputy Executive Director at the Coalition for Juvenile Justice, commented that between 50% and 75% of the incarcerated children in this country suffer from mental health problems. According to Gannon, very often, a fine line pointing to racial profiling and poverty separates juvenile offenders from other-children who are recognized, diagnosed, and treated in other settings. Even if children are properly diagnosed, not enough services may be available. Dr. Paree Stivers stated, "Mental health services have been geared toward seriously or chronically mentally ill adults, but there are not enough services for families and extended family members." Betty Carley, a 30-year child welfare veteran from Florida, remarked, "Funding is limited; preventing early intervention to ward off the progression of more serious illnesses [in children]."

In the past, workers knew less about the recognition and treatment of many mental health problems. Responsible child welfare work now requires an understanding of how to recognize early signs of mental illness and substance abuse in children and families, so that intervention can be started before more serious problems develop. On-the-job training on these issues is often superficial, but workers can be blamed for not knowing what they have not been taught.

Child and adolescent suicide continues to be a grave concern for child welfare advocates. The most recent National Center for Injury Prevention (1998) report stated that over the past several decades, the suicide rate in young people has increased dramatically. In 1997, suicide was the third leading cause of death in 10- to 14-year-olds (with four times as many males as females). A startling 21% of high school students had contemplated suicide in the past year, and 8% had tried to kill themselves (National Center for Injury Prevention, 1998). Again, early recognition and intervention of these problems often fall to workers, along with responsibility for searching out reliable resources.

Drug Abuse

Another lagging area for kids is in drug abuse and treatment. The Substance Abuse and Mental Health Services Administration (SAMHSA) indicates that 1.1 million children 12 to 17 years old have problems with drugs and alcohol, but only about 122,000 children with substance abuse problems received treatment in 2000 (Leinwand, 2002). According to Mitchell Rosenthal, head of Phoenix House Foundation, "those kids are only the tip of the [drug abuse] iceberg." CPS workers and substance abuse counselors struggle to find treatment because a national shortage of adequate adolescent drug rehabilitation centers exists. Even if they do find a rehabilitation center, they worry about relapse, and relapse prevention is a priority.

In addition, thousands of children are growing up with caregivers who are drug or alcohol abusers. These kids are at higher risk for becoming addicted later on and can be psychologically affected.

Internet and Media Violence

Escalating TV and movie violence is desensitizing children and possibly contributing to their violent behavior. The Internet is also becoming a potentially dangerous place for kids. Workers must remain vigilant about child molesters who use this new technology for victimizing children. Dealing with the fallout that occurs when children have been victimized by predators through the Internet is a newer aspect of the child welfare worker's job (Blom, 1998).

Gun Violence

Sadly, gun violence continues to be another problem not easily solved but at the forefront of child welfare work. Every day in America, nine children are killed by firearms. Nearly 1 million U.S. students took guns to school during 1998. Of teen suicides, 60% involve guns—nearly 3,000 teens kill themselves with guns each year. Most astonishingly, gunshot wounds to children ages 16 and younger have increased 300% in major urban areas since 1986 (OJJDP, 1999). Guns not only endanger children, they add a lethal dimension to the child welfare worker's job.

Challenge Four—Understanding New Research

In the 1990s, aptly referred to as the "decade of the brain," researchers made significant inroads with regard to neuroscience and understanding why children behave the way they do. Therefore, knowing about posttraumatic stress disorder (PTSD) and other biological disorders in children has become part of child welfare work. Research points to physical or psychological trauma as the cause of many children's problems. Child advocates need to know how to handle a child when his or her fight or flight responses are triggered, because most children placed in protective services experience these feelings.

Child welfare workers are not only working with traumatized children and families, but are also attempting to work with traumatized communities. One Native American worker in the northwest reported:

> I am afraid to work in my community because it is becoming so dangerous. If my family and I speak out against sexual or drug abuse, some of our tribal members become angry. I don't blame them entirely. We've been traumatized for decades because we were displaced and then denied our traditions. I cry when I think about my grandmother who went to her grave without being allowed to hear the drumming of her ancestors. Oppression is terrible and creates so much trauma.

Workers must understand scientific studies related to prevention, diagnosis, and treatment, because these studies can guide them in designing better treatment plans. As some workers reported, they cannot assume that doctors or administrators already have this information when they present cases at team meetings. As one worker commented, "I was surprised at how little our consulting psychiatrist knew about the impact of traumatic experiences on neural biology. I have to be really careful not to bruise his ego in staff meetings, but quite honestly, it's a challenge."

Challenge Five—Worker Compensation

Clearly, the 21st century presents complex challenges to child welfare workers. These days, workers must be better trained, flexible, culturally sensitive, and emotionally capable. To fulfill these new job requirements, workers need to be compensated in a variety of ways. Gaensbauer and Wamboldt (2000) reported that "intensive staff-training programs, competitive salaries, and a comprehensive staff development plan are crucial to promote staff competence and to reduce staff turnover. To facilitate family empowerment, staff empowerment is necessary." These are not new or unreasonable conclusions.

Training

Nancy Gannon, in Washington, DC, feels there is room for a lot of improvement:

> *Training and job orientation has [sic] changed. So much of it is now oriented to technical issues, rather than professional practice. There were more resources, especially with regard to training and supervision opportunities when I began working in this field.*

Home Safe Director Jill Kinney said, "There is less training and consultation from outside support than in the past." Kinney echoed many veteran workers who remember the 1970s and 1980s as decades that stressed and financed outside continuing education for child welfare workers.

Salaries

Competitive salary is a relative term among child advocates. Considering the job requirements and comparing them with other professions can be unsettling for even the most altruistic workers. For example, the *1999 National Employment Statistics Report* (Bureau of Labor Statistics, 2000) revealed that community and social services occupations were paid $14.01 an hour, or a $31,640 mean annual income. Comparing that with teachers, who averaged $40,000 per year and $44,000 in 2002 can be frustrating.

The Bureau of Labor Statistics (2000) broke down community and social services jobs into more specific occupations and wages (see Table 1). Child care workers are listed in the personal care and service occupations category and earn $6.91 per hour, for an annual income of $15,000. Foster parents receive $12 to $20 per day for each child, compared with boarding facilities that receive $12 to $20 per day for boarding a pet!

When the majority of community and social services occupations require college degrees, it can be discouraging to compare them with other professions, such as the life, physical, and social science category, which reflect similar educational backgrounds. The mean hourly wage for those professions is $20.00 per hour and $45,660 annually. Foresters receive a reported annual income of $42,020 per year, and chemical technicians receive $36,080.

In another job category in which a bachelor's or master's degree is not required, installation, maintenance, and repair, tire changers receive $18,630 annually, whereas home appliance repairers earn $30,020. Machine maintenance workers receive $31,800 yearly, and automotive body repairers earn $33,720. This begs the question: Why does our society place less monetary value on caring for its children than repairing its vehicles or boarding its animals?

Table I

National Employment Statistics for Community and Social Services Occupations

Occupation	Average Annual Salary
Substance abuse and behavioral disorder counselor	$28,560
Child, family, and school social worker	$31,720
Mental health and substance abuse social worker	$31,150
Social and human services assistant	$22,760

Source: Adapted from Bureau of Labor Statistics (1999).

Current child welfare salaries have not increased with tougher job responsibilities. A possible explanation may be that conventional public thinking about child advocacy might relate to times when working in behalf of kids was overseen by missionaries or other spiritually motivated individuals. Whatever the reason, perhaps we could learn from teachers' unions, which have made some inroads with regard to public relations and financial compensation.

Challenge Six—Avoiding Worker Burnout

Many talented child advocates have left their jobs for reasons that include job requirements, low pay, and insufficient supervision. Contrary to conventional public perception, child advocates are human and do not have continuous wells of empathy or energy. The work can be tough, and without financial and emotional support people will leave.

If we want to dissuade workers from leaving their jobs, child welfare must become integrated as a value within our society. The general public is concerned about protecting kids, but this concern seems attached to an attitude that suggests, "It's someone else's job."

Shay Bilchik, President/CEO of the Child Welfare League of America, stated:

> *The public needs to take collective ownership of children*
> *and understand that kids in need are not too different*

from their own. Child welfare needs to be seen as part of the larger systemic picture, not isolated from the rest of society.

The tired argument that more money is spent on our country's defense than on the health and well-being of our children sadly continues to be true. Federal and state child welfare budgets consistently reflect low investment in the protection of children. Child welfare leaders have tried to gain the public's attention, while federal and state bureaucrats diligently work to responsibly distribute limited funding. At times, however, this appears to be a losing battle.

Money is not the only issue, and ill-spent funds cannot transform child welfare either. Politicians need to understand that decisions beginning at the legislative level often start a chain of events that cause problems in the future. For example, if a bill that funds mental health treatment to youth in detention fails, citizens may later pay a price as crime victims or prison underwriters.

Worker burnout occurs when people are overwhelmed by their responsibilities, and child welfare work is no exception. Societal problems that contribute to child abuse and neglect have become too complex to be solved solely by child welfare workers. Legislators, prompted by a public outcry, have the potential to reevaluate tired approaches to funding and accountability in the child welfare system. A shift toward enacting proactive prevention projects in behalf of kids could prevail over building jails. Losing good child welfare workers to these complex, sometimes overwhelming challenges can be avoided if we all assume more responsibility for the safety and well-being of our children.

Do We Have a Child Welfare Crisis?

America's child welfare system has been in crisis for a while now. Charlotte McCullough believes that "crisis in child welfare" has become a belabored phrase. She stated, "Every year the media headlines the crisis in our country. But things haven't changed. We need to fix tomorrow's crisis by making a long-term strategic effort to change these conditions."

McCullough seems to be on to something. She raises some good questions. Are child welfare workers willing to accept the child welfare crisis as a permanent condition in America? Has the crisis in child welfare become

How Can We Cope with Mounting Challenges?

Everyone wants to feel safe and secure. When change occurs at work, we may feel unsteady for a while. Here are some suggestions that can help. They are intended to draw on personal strengths and help us become less affected by stressors.

- Begin to assume that change happens with any job.

- Write down the following questions with your dominant hand, then answer them using your nondominant hand. You may be surprised by the responses.

    - What do I believe about change?

    - What do I tell myself about who I am when I become disappointed by someone's change in behavior?

    - How do I cope when my supervisor announces changes in paperwork and other procedures?

    - Would I like to cope differently with regard to job rules and regulation changes? If so, in what way?

    - Examine how you can improve your skills, even if you have a lot of experience.

- Changes at work can sometimes be met with resentment. Think about how they are introduced before judging their viability. Sometimes, presentations get in the way of the message. If the presentation is the problem, offer suggestions about how to make it easier to hear.

- Examine your opinion before sharing, but try to share it.

- Politics on the job can work to our advantage. Think about becoming involved through committee participation at work or taking time alone with an administrator. Most supervisors appreciate enthusiastic input. Work at being visible. Do not be hesitant about getting involved in the political process. Politicians listen to people who help them win elections.

- Let go of any illusions that things will "go back to the way they were." It doesn't happen. Our ability to adapt to change is one of the best human qualities.

- Examine your physical response when you are required to make changes at work. Does your body tense? Is your breathing affected? Instead of responding to your body's danger signals, ask yourself, "What's going on? Am I in danger? Is anything really happening to me?" Drink cold water. Then, lace your fingers together, place them over your stomach, and take deep breaths.

- Under the best of circumstances, we can get flustered. The manner in which we work through our feelings is the real challenge. Take a hot bath, go to the gym, or privately kick an empty cardboard box in the backyard to reduce tension.

confused in the public's mind with "normal"? Answers will be revealed in this new century.

In Spite of Challenges, People Still Become Child Advocates

In spite of the challenges, the majority of us advocate for kids because of our desire to do good. All my life people have come to me to talk. I guess I'm a good listener. For me, family and equality are very important. We need to look out for others. And I can't do that as well working in a travel agency," comments a 35-year veteran.

In his book, Parent (1996) commented:

> I know in my heart that I've saved the lives of many children. It's hard to describe the way I feel when I think about that. As soon as I'm about to say anything, the complexity of it overwhelms me. Satisfaction begins to tap it— there's more, but I just can't find the words for it. At the very bottom of me, a place I don't go to very often, there's satisfaction and I think it has something to do with the kids who are walking the planet because of the efforts I

made at crucial points in their lives. I never feel proud about the good things I managed to do at Emergency Children's Services. I don't spend much time patting my back about it all. It was my job.

Child welfare work is as much a call to service as it is a job. One worker explained it this way: "I know I'm doing what I'm supposed to be doing." Many feel that no other career offers the opportunities to share of oneself in such a lasting, meaningful way.

Although outward signs point to discouraging facts about current working conditions, people will continue to enter the child welfare field, because they have the capacity to see beyond the superficial. Child welfare workers are determined to work for the well-being of children, even when it means placing ourselves in harm's way. In the end, we want to serve. And through this act of service, we sometimes work miracles.

References

Blom, E. (1998, October 11). Danger online: Child abusers exploit new opportunities via Internet. *Maine Telegram*, 1A.

Braithwaite, E. R. (1962). *Paid servant.* New York: McGraw-Hill.

Bureau of Labor Statistics, U.S. Department of Labor. (2000). *1999 national occupational employment and wage estimates.* Washington, DC: Author.

Child Welfare League of America. (1999). *CWLA Standards of excellence for services for abused or neglected children and their families.* Washington, DC: Author.

Ehrenreich, B. (2001). *Nickel and dimed: On (not) getting by in America.* New York: Henry Holt.

Gaensbauer, T., & Wamboldt, M. (2000, January). *Proposal for CPS and CCAPS statement regarding gun violence.* Available from http://aacap.org/info_families/nationalfacts/cogunviol.htm.

Leinwand, D. (2002, February 7). Youth need more drug programs, study shows. *USA Today.*

Levy, T. M., & Orlans, M. (1998). *Attachment, trauma, and healing: Understanding and treating attachment disorder in children and families.* Washington, DC: CWLA Press.

Meckler, L. (2001, May 22). Child well-being on upswing in U.S. *Portsmouth Herald*, 1.

National Center for Injury Prevention & Control. (1998). *Suicide prevention fact sheet*. Washington, DC: Author.

Office of Juvenile Justice and Delinquency Prevention. (1999). *Justice Policy Institute Report youth arrest data for 1999*. Washington, DC: Author.

Parent, M. (1996). *Turning stones: A caseworker's story: My days and nights with children at risk*. New York: Harcourt Brace.

Additional Resources

Bernstein, N. (2002, July 29). Side effect of welfare law: The no-parent family. *The New York Times*, 1.

Bryan, S. M. (2003, February 1). One job doesn't pay the bills. *Albuquerque Journal*, 8.

Robert Wood Johnson Foundation. (2002). *The health care group*. Washington, DC: Author.

CHAPTER 2

Utilizing Neuroscience in Child Welfare Work

I Thought I Didn't Have to Take Science!

> Developmental experiences determine the capability of the
> brain to do things. If you don't change those developmen-
> tal experiences, you're not going to change the hardware of
> the brain and we'll end up building more prisons.
> —*Bruce Perry, neural psychiatrist*

Discuss scientific terms with most child welfare workers and their eyes begin
to cross. Many workers would say that they are interested in understanding
relationships, not brains. But brain research gives them an advantage when
addressing the needs of children. Discoveries made in neural science in the
1990s make it easier for child welfare workers to set realistic goals when
planning interventions. Understanding this research is part of the job
description. Still, any researcher would say much research is still to be done
before the brain is fully understood. That is probably why the 21st century
has also been called the "millennium of the brain."

The terms on the following page illustrate current usage in neurobiologi-
cal research.

Thirty years ago, people who worked in child welfare knew a lot less about
the role environment plays on a developing brain. Since then, dedicated

Neurobiological Definitions for Research (see Figure 1)

Neuron—A nerve cell that underlies the basis for brain formation. Babies have more than 1 billion at birth. They receive, analyze, coordinate, and transmit information.

Synapses—Connections that organize the brain by forming neuronal pathways to parts of the brain. They can grow stronger with learning and weaken or disappear when not used.

Neurotransmitters—Brain chemicals that enable cells to talk to each other about what is going on around and within us. Neurotransmitters jump across gaps between cells.

Serotonin—A neurotransmitter that regulates impulses for emotions and keeps aggression in check. If serotonin levels fall, violence rises, including in children. Low levels of serotonin may cause depression, bad temper, and explosive rage.

Noradrenaline—This alarm hormone compels the brain to respond to danger, producing adrenaline and other chemicals that prepare the body for fight or flight. It is thought that an imbalance of noradrenaline may create impulsive violence.

Dendrites—Fibers extending from the body of the neuron which receive incoming signals from other neurons.

Axon—A fiber that conveys outgoing impulses to other cells. There can be many dendrites in a neuron but only one axon or arm.

Cortex—One of the last regions of the brain to develop, the cortex is involved in abstract thinking.

Plasticity—Refers to how the brain can create, strengthen, or discard synapses and neuronal pathways in response to the environment.

Amygdala—An almond-shaped region in the brain that is part of the limbic system, which imparts fear. One of the amygdala's main jobs is to tell people what things are scary and what should be avoided. It also plays a role in registering reward.

Limbic system—Located in the lower midbrain, it connects to key parts such as the hippocampus and cerebral cortex, where abstract thinking occurs. The limbic system sorts through sensory input as well as thoughts and identifies whether they are good, bad, or neutral. Emotions generated here help us adapt to the environment.

Hippocampus—An area of the brain involved in learning and memory. It is responsible for making associations and plays a role in conscious memory. It also consolidates memories.

Adrenaline—A stress hormone that responds to psychological or physical danger and prepares the body for fight or flight.

Cortisol—A stress hormone that responds to psychological or physical danger and prepares the body for fight or flight. It regulates sleep/wake cycles, mental arousal, and the immune system. It can also affect our ability to speak.

Dopamine—A neuron that regulates emotions on one part of the brain and motor control in another.

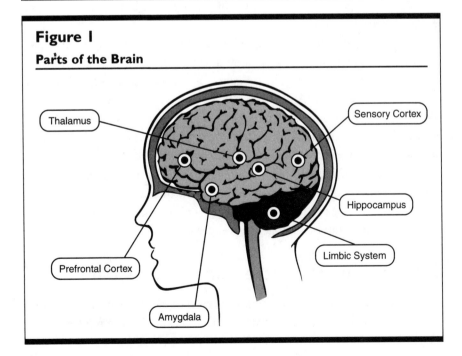

Figure 1
Parts of the Brain

researchers have accomplished tremendous feats, due to their implementation of brain imaging tools. Scientists now know that the brain is more elastic than once thought and that what happens to a child in the womb through age 3 determines a good deal about how he or she grows and develops. In the past decade, a beginning understanding of altered brain functioning resulting from early abuse and neglect has emerged.

It is now evident that genetics provides a predisposition for children to develop in certain ways, but interactions in the environment have a major effect on how children's predispositions will be expressed. These interactions organize the brain's development and, thus, shape the people we become (National Clearinghouse, 2001). Genetics and environment work together to influence children's growth and development.

Genetics: One Side of the Coin

Most people would prefer to blame health and behavior problems on genes. It is human nature to blame something we have no control over. Although Huntington's disease, a progressive neurodegenerative disorder that causes deterioration of motor, cognitive, and memory functioning, is almost totally genetic, the majority of diseases are both genetically and environmentally influenced.

Genes are now linked to eating disorders, autism, attention deficit/hyperactivity disorder (ADHD), and other mental health problems. Although schizophrenia is partly caused by genes, it can be generated by environmental factors as well (Andreasen, 2001). Some mental illnesses are more influenced by environmental factors, such as exposure to head and birth injuries, viral infections, hormonal changes, drug or alcohol abuse, vaccinations, stress, toxic chemicals, and malnutrition.

Andreasen (2001) states that our genetic code is not as rigid as once thought: "Genes do not contain a static and unchanging set of instructions....Rather, they modify their influences on the body in response to their own 'environmental' or 'non-genetic' experiences."

Environment: The Other Side of the Coin

Most children in the CPS system have been shaped as much by their exposure to substance abuse, poverty, violence, and absentee parenting as by their genes. Both behaviorists and biological scientists share the opinion that today's societal conditions have created a negative effect on the health and well-being of children.

Immediately following birth, the brain has a huge growth spurt, constructing trillions of neural connections. The brain self-organizes, awaiting new experiences that create networks for learning, including reasoning, problem solving, building character values, and learning language and rational thinking. These essential networks are formed by age 1 and help us make associations and think abstractly, laying the foundation for future intelligence, imagination, and creativity. But these networks can be aborted when early childhood experiences lack mental stimulation or are stressful (Kotulak, 1996).

Researchers have found that another environmental brain builder is the spoken language. The number of words a child hears daily boosts her or his intelligence, social skills, and scholastic achievements. Conversely, a lack of words stunts the brain. Words need to come from a caregiver who speaks with love and meaning, not from the radio or television.

Kotulak (1996) contributes that listening to certain types of music helps the brain in "connecting the information dots." One study showed that adult male musicians had more brain matter than male nonmusicians. Some of our parents knew what they were doing when they required us to take piano lessons.

Environment makes a big difference in the way children learn and grow. Child welfare workers are equipped with more than enough evidence to use this information in taking an active role when it comes to guiding caregivers and intervening in behalf of injured youth. "Wait and see" is no longer an intervention strategy, because time is of the essence when it comes to helping a young mind.

Prenatal Experiences Affect Children's Brains

Researchers have discovered that malnutrition both before and after birth results in stunted brain growth and slower passage of electrical signals in the brain. The most common form of malnutrition is iron deficiency, resulting in cognitive and motor delays, anxiety, depression, and social and attention problems. Protein deficiency can cause motor and cognitive delays and impulsive behavior. Even if the nutritional problems are repaired, it may be difficult to change cognitive and behavioral impairments (Kotulak, 1996).

A baby's brain formation can also be changed by exposure to drugs and alcohol. Drugs can alter development of the cortex in the brain, and they can reduce the number of neurons that are created. In addition, mothers who abuse drugs and alcohol affect the way their babies' chemical messages are understood (National Clearinghouse, 2001). Not all children exposed in utero develop problems as a result of their mothers' excessive use of substances, but they can develop fetal alcohol syndrome; mental retardation; and attention, memory, problem-solving, and abstract thinking difficulties.

Extreme stress in mothers during pregnancy may also affect newborns. A mother's physically or emotionally stressful experiences can cause stress hormones to become overactive in the baby, creating abnormal connections among the child's brain cells. Consequently, the brain can learn things incorrectly, later creating learning problems and depression (Kotulak, 1996).

Studies suggest that mothers who report high levels of stress during their pregnancies may also risk having children who are hyperactive or developmentally delayed. One researcher remarked,

> If you think about the fact that the inner city population is chronically stressed and there's a lot of that population chronically pregnant, then we can begin to see some of the biology that may be responsible for high rates of aggression in the children. (Kotulak, 1996)

All of this research suggests that reassuring support provided by professional and nonprofessionals workers can help. For instance, natural helpers, such as neighbors, can be drawn into coaching mothers at risk before and after their pregnancies.

Positive Stimulation Helps Newborns and Infants

Research is discovering information about the effects of brain stimulation. In a University of Washington study, Geraldine Dawson found that about 40% of infants born to depressed mothers had reduced electrical activity in their emotion centers. By age 3, they were more likely to be withdrawn, disobedient, and aggressive. The children also had high levels of stress hormones, were apt to cry, and experienced sleep disturbances. Depression frequently causes inhibition in expression and interaction. Mothers affected by this mood disorder may not have the ability to provide stimulation to their babies as well as mothers who are not depressed.

Lack of infant stimulation is most often seen in babies who fail to thrive. These children, however, are at the extreme end of the spectrum. Many children have their basic food and shelter needs met, but are left alone or otherwise ignored. Children with severe sensory deprivation risk developing smaller brains as the cortex (the region associated with abstract thinking) can develop abnormally.

For children to master developmental tasks, they need to be exposed to opportunities. A difference exists between what a baby absorbs in a playpen versus when taking an outing with his or her mother or father. Exposure to textures, sounds, laughter, hugs, pleasant voices, cooing, colors, the outdoors, patterning by exercising little legs and arms, and lots of encouragement and affirmation are brain food for babies.

Infants also need face-to-face contact to make sounds that form words and pull together sentences. Many well-intentioned parents place their children in carriers and go about transporting them with little or no interaction. Missed opportunities abound, even with busy parents who have the best of intentions.

Without the right emotional input, an infant's brain does not receive the proper signals that inspire it to create neural networks that have positive emotional patterns. The input consists of reinforced joy and pleasure. If a child is not properly stimulated, the brain will begin to prune pathways that carry information to various parts of the brain, affecting the recognition and expression of emotions. Researchers report that although experiences may alter and change the functioning of an adult, they literally provide the organizing framework for an infant and child (National Clearinghouse, 2001). As they say in neuroscience, "If you don't use it, you lose it."

Infants and babies who are not stimulated by kindness or demonstrations of love may have their ability to show goodwill and connect with others later impaired. If young brains are not patterned by demonstration and experience, then they do not create pathways that register and carry information. Researchers have found that children learn empathy through imitation. Dr. Jean Decety said, "By imitation we may feel what another person

Ashes to Ashes

Dust to Dust

Oil those Brains

Before they Rust.

—Anonymous (1996)

felt, which is the very definition of human empathy." Is it any surprise that children from abusive and neglectful homes are socially or emotionally immature?

Research has also shown that a young brain is malleable and can be changed with positive stimulation. Have you ever wondered why preschoolers learn other languages and new skills so easily? Their brains are more elastic, and they can build neural connections faster than older people. Child advocates have an opportunity to witness change in their young clients because early intervention is key to helping abused and neglected kids.

Adjusting Our Approach

Child advocates might feel that applying this new brain research is both exciting and discouraging. Armed with information about infant stimulation, we can guide new mothers toward programs that help in developing their children's minds. Yet, it can be disheartening to recognize that many of these same mothers have had little in the way of stimulating or nurturing backgrounds themselves. According to a Washington organization that studies social changes affecting children, Child Trends, Inc., 42% of U.S. families start out with some serious liabilities. They include mothers who have not finished high school at the birth of their babies, unmarried parents, and a lack of maturity in parents, such as mothers who are younger than 20 when they give birth for the first time. According to Child Trends (Kotulak, 1996), one new family in nine experiences all three factors. There is great need for infant stimulation programs and biologically enlightened day care centers.

New research points to the need for program directors to review and rewrite social policies to keep up with best practice that pertains to the brain. Training child welfare workers and advocates on how to apply biological research to their work must be a priority. Agencies should set aside funding to ensure this happens.

Stress Plays a Big Role in How the Young Brain Functions

Violence and Aggression

It's not surprising that aggressive and violent behaviors in children are linked to chronic stress and neglect. Prenatal, infant, and early childhood experiences provide the organizing framework for children's personalities and affect their ability to relate to others and cope with stress later. Children who have experienced chronic abuse and neglect can later become persistently hyperaroused, dissociative, or vigilant about their personal safety.

Serious conditions can also surface when children do not receive appropriate stimulation through exposure to positive experiences or emotional support. One of these conditions includes not feeling remorse when hurting others. Children so affected become emotionally retarded. The part of the brain that allows human beings to feel connected with others does not develop (National Clearinghouse, 2001).

Studies have also shown that threatening environments can trigger serotonin and noradrenaline (neural chemicals linked to violence and aggression) imbalances in genetically susceptible people. Schanberg said, "A stressful environment has caused genes important for survival to become overly expressed, making human beings more aggressive and violent" (as cited in Kotulak, 1996). Spring-boarding from that theme, Kotulak (1996) offered one example of just how many children are exposed to these environments when he reported that a Chicago study of 1,000 children from poor neighborhoods revealed that 74% had witnessed a murder, shooting, stabbing, or robbery. Nearly half of them were themselves victims of a rape, shooting, stabbing, robbery, or other violent act. In fact, although the U.S. population increased by 40% from 1960 through 1991, violent crime increased 560%. Increases in stressful conditions in our society are largely to blame.

Child workers must be mindful of the conditions created from ongoing stress, yet be aware that most children do not become violent as a result of their bad experiences. Our genes may provide part of the answer. Newer research has found a rare mutated gene that raises noradrenaline levels and increases impulsive aggression in men. Research has also found a mutated gene that may also lower serotonin levels, increasing aggression (Kotulak, 1996).

Stress and Memory

Memories are repeated experiences that strengthen neuronal pathways in the brain. Over time, these pathways become "sensitized" as memories. Three types of memories include motor memories, such as tying shoelaces; cognitive, such as "two plus two is four"; and emotional, "I'm happy!" When children are abused or neglected, they create negative neuronal pathways, establishing a foundation that may inhibit their later ability to respond to their environment in a positive way. If children's brains are not stimulated by appropriate early nurturing, acts of kindness can be met with confusion and anger, because sensitized memory pathways about a safe world have not been created. For example, many frustrated foster parents or extended family caregivers have given up when their efforts to nurture were met with hostility by their young wards.

Stress can affect a child's ability to remember and transmit information. When a child's cerebral cortex and limbic system register unsettling experiences, they sound an alarm to other parts of the body, preparing him or her to cope. Cortisol, a life-sustaining hormone, responds by playing an active role. It regulates the sleep/wake cycle, mental arousal, and the immune system, and it fills both the hippocampus and the amygdala, two areas of the brain linked to memory function. Researchers have identified abnormal secretions of cortisol in maltreated children (Andreasen, 2001).

McEwen found that chronic stress can eventually cause the neurons in the hippocampus to lose dendrites and spines, due to ongoing cortisol released during times of trouble. Consequently, the hippocampus can shrink in size, limiting this area's memory sorting and organizing functions.

After experiencing a traumatic event, our brains can theoretically forget or block memories. In *The Seven Sins of Memory*, Schacter (2002) explained that reports of temporary forgetting of sexual abuse by a family member are more common than reports of forgetting abuse by a non–family member.

Psychologists have theorized that because children are emotionally and physically dependent on their caregivers, they need to selectively remember nontraumatic memories. This adaptation allows the child to tolerate living with his or her family (Schacter, 2002).

Youth who remember childhood abuse later can experience something called "directed forgetting" Sometimes, perpetrators direct children to forget their abuse. As a result, kids will consciously avoid those memories, repeatedly inhibiting access to them. Strong cues or triggers later, however, can elicit emotions felt by the abuse survivor, and a memory will emerge. For example, a movie containing elements similar to personal experience may prompt the memory. Schooler documented a case involving a 30-year-old man who suddenly remembered being sexually molested at age 12 by a parish priest. Prior to watching a movie, he had no memory of the abuse. Severe stress can block out parts of our past, while allowing us to continue to form and maintain new information.

PET scans (positron-emission tomography) have shown that people with blocked memories have less activity in certain parts of the brain, substantiating abnormal brain function (Schacter, 2002). Neurochemical imbalances, abnormal brain structures, and information fed to the brain (creating neuronal pathways) have a lot to do with accessing or suppressing memories. These conditions also play a large part when it comes to being flooded with memories.

Children can be flooded by memories of their trauma when they experience nightmares or persistent intrusive thoughts. These conditions are deeply disturbing and difficult to control. As children try to manage their memories and anxiety, they may take drugs or distract themselves with other risky behaviors.

Chronic activation of neuronal pathways involved in the fear response can wear out certain areas and create permanent memories in the brain that shape the child's perception of and response to his or her environment, even after it improves. Therefore, although a child may currently live in a safe environment, she may continue to believe that she is not safe. Efforts to suppress these feelings raise anxiety (Schacter, 2002), and a vicious cycle that involves triggers, invasive thoughts, and attempts to control the physical and emotional feelings can emerge.

The False Memory Phenomenon

Child welfare workers have investigated sexual abuse reports for a long time. Essentially, they have endeavored to prove that children generally do not make up these disclosures. But as the profession succeeded in bringing this issue to light, scientific evidence surfaced about false memory.

Some of the more surprising brain research relates to the brain's ability to adapt memories or simply make them up. Some researchers believe that false memories are encoded at the time of an event. Others think a general picture or schema is constructed, and a later error occurs when reconstructing the past experience; untrue events consistent with the schema become part of the memory. Assigning a memory to the wrong source, such as mistaking fantasy for reality or misinterpreting the past, is called "misattribution."

Researchers have discovered that the brain is susceptible to suggestions in certain people. Experiments conducted at Western Washington University demonstrated researchers could successfully implant false memories in a significant minority of study participants. Those people scored higher on scales that measure vividness of visual imagery than participants who could not be successfully implanted (Schacter, 2002).

Right- and left-brain research has used the help of "split brain" patients to offer other information. It has been discovered that the left side of the brain will generate false reports. The left brain excels at developing schemata and has an ability to determine the source of a memory based on surrounding events. The right side of the brain is good at perception aspects of stimulus. The left brain constantly looks for order and reason when there is none, so it continues to make mistakes that include constructing a "potential" past as opposed to the true one (Damasio, 2002).

Loftus believes that some people may be so suggestible that they could be convinced they are responsible for crimes they did not commit. She said, "Much of what goes on—unwittingly—is contamination." McNally has studied false memory individuals who, when retaining a completely false memory, perspire and experience increased heart rate.

Fewer reports exist now than in the late 1980s and early 1990s regarding retrieved memories about sexual abuse, probably due to the fact that therapists and investigative interviewers are more careful in their approach to eliciting information from clients. Child welfare workers who intervene in behalf of youth who disclose sexual abuse must be trained to follow careful procedures as well as recognize appropriate evaluation skills by their colleagues. We must also remember that trauma can create false memories, and that most of the time, children do not fabricate sexual abuse.

Stress Can Create Mood Disorders in Children and Youth

A large number of children who enter the child welfare system experience some form of mood disorder, because excessive stress can interfere with the development of the subcortical and limbic systems and result in anxiety, depression, and the ability to form attachments.

Irritability in the limbic system can cause panic disorder and other conditions associated with posttraumatic stress. Workers often see these problems in juvenile detention jails, foster care, or treatment centers. The trouble begins in the brain when a child is stressed as a result of chronic abuse and neglect.

Serotonin is the neural transmitter that regulates impulse and emotion, including aggressive tendencies. Researchers have discovered abnormal levels in depressed and anxious people. Abnormal levels of noradrenaline, the accelerator neurotransmitter, can cause aggressive behavior as well.*

Siegle and his colleagues have studied one mood disorder in particular; depression. They reported that when depressed people read a list of depressing words, they had a different response in the amygdala than when the same words were read by nondepressed people. In depressed individuals, this region could be activated for as long as 25 seconds after hearing a depressing word. Nondepressed people stop showing activity after 10 seconds. It is suggested from this study that depressed people will think about sad words longer.

Diminished growth in the left hemisphere due to stress may also increase the risk for depression. Anxiety can also emerge when chronic traumatic stress causes sensitized pathways about fear and memory to be created.

Studies of patients with damage to the amygdala have shown that this region, required for fear conditioning and other aspects of emotional memory, can be affected. This area is activated during fear conditioning and can create unconscious fear memories (Damasio, 2002). Consequently, children may not be able to identify what triggers their intense reactions or anxiety.

---

* Researchers still disagree on the neurochemical imbalance model as a source of depression, and they continue to seek definitive answers.

Over time, the brain becomes sensitive to cues that represent possible danger, and an automatic fear response may occur. This fear response is called *hyperarousal*, and the brain's acute attunement to danger cues is called *hypervigilance*. When the fear response is triggered, freezing, withdrawal, and aggression can surface in children. Even subtle reminders of a traumatic experience can cause a child to feel anxious, causing a fear response.

Stress and Dissociation

Have you ever tried to speak with a young trauma survivor and felt invisible because you were ignored? Your perceptions could be right, because the child you are speaking to is experiencing dissociation and you could be the trigger, just because you may symbolically represent an authority figure. Dissociation, or the *surrender response*, occurs as an outgrowth of not receiving help during a traumatic experience. When help is not forthcoming, a child will "freeze," or become motionless, compliant, and eventually dissociative. Sensitized neural pathways create physical and mental freezing in a child, causing further anxiety and dissociation. Dissociation contributes to learning disabilities and hinders normal academic and social growth in children.

Children, Stress, and Relationships

National Clearinghouse (2001) said that lower brain responses become dominant and cognitive regulating structures do not develop to their full capacity when relationships are negative or weak. A youngster may not fully develop the ability to understand and control emotions or have awareness about other's emotions. This lack of empathy is a big part of the problem in children with attachment disorders.

Stress Can Affect Learning

Incorporating new information is difficult for many hyperaroused, traumatized children. Merzenich said, "We can now see how a learning disability could arise from a child's bad experiences." As a result of experiencing great fear, an imbalance in neurochemicals, as well as changes in the brain's formation, can occur. The body may assume an anxious state. According to Perry, it is not unusual for smart children to have difficulty learning and to be diagnosed with disabilities when they have experienced disturbing events. The definitions on the following page show the three major types of learning disabilities. Teachers know that children need to be in a state of "attentive calm" to assimilate new information. Social workers know the same thing about kids and social situations.

Stress Can Affect Children's Immune Systems

Stress hormones released from the brain, cortisol from the adrenal gland, and nerve chemicals all regulate immune cells to fight infection. Elevated levels of stress hormones contribute to a less effective immune system.

Individuals exposed to stress at the same time they are exposed to a cold virus showed more viral particles and produce more mucus than non-stressed people. In addition, people who are vaccinated during stressful periods may not develop full antibody protection. It has also been found that stress prolongs wound healing.

Animal studies show that social and physical stress can effect viruses such as herpes and influenza as well as affecting the course of viral illness, bacterial disease, and septic shock. Studies of people exposed to chronic social stresses for more than two months increase the susceptibility to the common cold. Long-term caregivers, such as foster parents with special-needs children, can develop blunted immune systems. People who experience marital problems are also at risk (Sternberg & Gold, 2002).

This information can be easily translated to the many health problems seen in maltreated children. Positive and supportive social networks along with group psychotherapy can enhance immune response and increase resistance to diseases, including cancer. Plugging kids into alternative programs that focus on skill and confidence building is essential. In addition, accessing respite care for weary caregivers can maintain a consistent stream of competent child welfare workers.

What Should We Do with this Research?

Does this neural research mean that our dreams and even our most poetic thoughts come down to chemistry? Neuroscientists are working on that. In the meantime, prompted by this dynamic new information, we have a lot to do. Working with children encourages us to be change agents for early intervention and recovery. Until researchers develop specific gene treatments, pediatric psychiatrists, with professional and volunteer child advocates, must address the problems that arise due to child abuse and neglect.

Learning Disabilities

Learning disabilities can be divided into three broad categories:

Developmental speech and language disorders include difficulty producing speech sounds, using spoken language to communicate, or understanding what other people say. They include developmental articulation disorder, developmental expressive language disorder, and developmental receptive language disorder.

Academic skills disorder, also known as dyslexia, affects 2% to 8% of elementary school children. The various types include developmental reading disorder, developmental writing disorder, and developmental arithmetic disorder.

Other learning disabilities include delays acquiring language, academic, and motor skills that can affect the ability to learn, but do not meet the criteria for a specific learning disability. Also included are coordination disorders, which can lead to poor penmanship, as well as certain spelling and memory disorders. Attention disorders are included in this category. In a large portion of affected children, hyperactivity accompanies the attention disorder. Attention disorders are not considered learning disabilities but they can interfere with school performance.

Early childhood programs can change the way kids grow and relate in the world. As a matter of fact, parents of younger adopted children have reported more change than parents who have adopted older kids. Vulnerable children who received services from 4 months to 5 years old showed better cognitive development than children who receive services from ages 5 to 8, with even more difference from children ages 12 to 18.

Our first task is educating ourselves and searching out training that informs us about current research. We need guidance about intervention techniques that bring about change in child and youth brain function. Keeping in mind that traumatized children need stability, predictability, nurturing, and understanding to transform their lives, additional suggestions follow.

Healing a Damaged Brain: A Strategy for Workers

Healing interventions must activate brain areas that have been altered and address the entire life of a child. Weekly therapy sessions alone do not do the job. To heal the brain, a child's routine must incorporate consistent and frequent replacement exercises, so that new neural pathways about safety, predictability, and nurturing are reinforced. The following case example illustrates how new routines can help children recover from trauma.

A Daily Recovery Schedule for Children in Care

Jennifer is a 10-year-old who experienced maltreatment and was placed in foster care. A recovery schedule for her could include a 7:00 a.m. wake up and a pleasant morning greeting as she and her foster dad make her bed together before eating a nutritious breakfast. After breakfast, supportive comments and good wishes send Jennifer off to her next environment, usually school or another type of structured setting. Education can address any learning problems and include supervised social and interactive exercises. Music, art, and dance would be part of the curriculum. Physical education would include team building, limb strengthening, and motor coordination activities.

Afternoon activities might include individual or group therapy with a mental health professional who works to engage both sides of her client's young brain by sand tray, art, metaphorical story telling, or eye movement desensitization reprocessing therapies. Other afterschool activities include age-appropriate fun, such as playing ball or house, working on a hobby, or even assisting with dinner preparation. Dinner engages all family members, and the family makes it a ceremony by offering a prayer or thanksgiving comment. After dinner, the family shares cleaning up, and caregivers assist with homework assignments and guide bath and bedtime preparation, leaving one hour free for Jennifer to watch safe television, call friends, or play outside. A goodnight ritual helps comfort Jennifer before the nightlight gets turned on.

Applying new research to child welfare work can be accomplished in many ways. As you consider your interventions, keep in mind the following interventions for parents and professionals:

- Children need to rehearse to learn new skills. If a child has no frame of reference about brushing his or her teeth, he or she will be less likely to pick up a toothbrush after only one demonstration. Neural pathways containing new information must be reinforced again and again.

- Children need mentoring to explore new opportunities that stimulate learning. Demonstrating and engaging in chores together is much more effective than giving direction and expecting a child to follow through.

- Parents need to encourage children to take healthy risks to explore the world. This means that caregivers create building blocks of safety so that children gradually get used to the idea that new experiences will not harm them. For example, safely catching a child prepares him or her to jump in a pool later on.

- Praise stimulates brain activity and prepares the child to view the world in healthy ways while instilling confidence. Too often, we have heard people ruin a brain-building moment when they add just one more phrase after praising their children. For example, "You did a great job, considering you're not that bright to begin with." Negative feedback stops developmental advances in kids.

- Remember to speak to infants and babies. Continue the habit even as children grow older, because you will be helping build a better brain.

- Remember to make time for children. "Time poverty" is a great enemy in building healthy brains and covers all social and economic groups. Some unstructured playtime for parents and children is needed. Do not over-structure time.

- Lobby for quality day care. Studies have shown that children can thrive in positive day care settings because they have opportunities to interact and be stimulated to learn in a variety of ways.

- Be a good role model. Be consistent with rewards and fair play and demonstrate healthy living. Many people say they are child advocates but eat junk food, use foul language, lie, lose their tempers, and smoke in front of children. Imitation is powerful. Role modeling can make a big difference in children's lives.

- Accentuate the positive and use humor to reframe experiences. We can fall into the habit of taking life too seriously. Remember, a wet towel is not the same as a mugging.

- Take time for yourself. Burned-out workers are less effective.

- Television is not a four-letter word. Used correctly, the right type of programs can stimulate and engage children in very positive ways. *Sesame Street* and *The Lion King* have done a lot to help build brain power. The key is being aware of programming.

- Positive touch is important. Hugs, pats, gentle wrestling, and snuggling are essential when stimulating neural connections.

- Share articles about healthy nurturing with caregivers. Put together brochures and spread the news about the power of good parenting and its effect on the brain. Do not wait for your agency to come up with something fancy. Put something together and pass it out (after you have received the okay from your supervisor). While you are at it, mail the information to legislators and other funders.

- Start a smoking cessation program with parents.

- Initiate support groups for parents that address infant and child stimulation.

- Be a role model for parents and offer them opportunities to experience healthy ways to celebrate and begin rituals in their families. Use natural helpers in the community such as neighbors, church groups, and local volunteers to spread the news about the importance of creating safe living skills and routines.

- Create respite care for foster parents and birthparents. Play groups, substitute caregivers, parenting exchanges, and organized outings give a break to people in need of rest and nurturing.

- Examine your expectations about how children should respond to you. At the same time, review any biases you may have against medication or psychotherapy. Review your past and see if there are triggers that cause you to become hyperaroused or hypervigilant on the job.

• Remember that the brain is an organ, and when it becomes damaged, it needs physical rehabilitation, such as the introduction and repetition of new, more useful material.

Researchers Have Made a Significant Contribution

Child welfare workers are beginning to recognize the tremendous contribution neural researchers have made to our field. Without neural research, we might expect kids that will get over their anger, ignore their reading problems, and snap out of their flashbacks. Neural research has provided a larger picture by explaining why children behave the way they do.

Neuroscience has established that

• environment affects brain development,

• intelligence is not determined at birth,

• development of certain abilities is more efficient during specific growth periods,

• emotions can affect learning ability, and

• strong emotions affect memory and may decrease thought processes.

Empowered by this information, we are prepared to do a better job in behalf of children and families in the 21st century.

References

Andreasen, N. C. (2001). *The brave new brain: Conquering mental illness in the era of the genome.* New York: Oxford Press.

Anonymous. (1996). In J. Prelutsky (Ed.), *A nonny mouse writes again!: Poems.* Econo-Clad Books.

Damasio, A. R. (2002, August 31). How the brain creates the mind. *Scientific American; Special Edition,* 4–9.

Kotulak, R. (1996). Inside the brain: Revolutionary discoveries of how the mind works. Kansas City, MO: Andrews McMeel.

National Clearinghouse on Child Abuse and Neglect Information, (2001, October 1). *Understanding the effects of maltreatment on early brain development.* Available from http://calib.com/nccanch/pubs/infocus.cfm.

Schacter, D. L. (2002). *The seven sins of memory: How the mind forgets and remembers.* New York: Houghton Mifflin.

Sternberg, E. M., & Gold, P. W. (2002, August 31). The mind-body interaction in disease. *Scientific American*, 82–89.

Additional Resources

Appenzeller, T. (2002, July 1). The musical mind: If song has no purpose, why is it deep-wired in the brain? *U.S. News & World Report*, 60–61.

Blum, D. (1997). *Sex on the brain: The biological differences between men and women.* New York: Penguin Books.

Bremner, J. D. (1999). *Traumatic memories lost and found: Can lost memories of abuse be found in the brain?* Thousand Oaks, CA: Sage.

Brown, A. B. (n.d.). PTSD: A biological response gone awry? *NARSAD Research Newsletter.* Available from http://www.narsad.org/pub/win02ptsd.html.

Decraene, M. (2002, June). Postnatal pampering. *Psychology Today, 35*(3).

False memories easy to induce, study shows. (2003, February 24). *Florida Times Union*, C6.

Gloomy Gus might blame brain. (2002, February 17). *Times Union.*

Goldstein, A. (2000, July 3). Paging all parents. *Time Magazine*, 47.

Goode, E. (2002, June 18). Physically abused children recognize face of anger. *New York Times*, D4.

Greem, S. C., & Wonderlich, S., (1999, June). *Psychological effects of childhood sexual abuse.* Fargo, ND: Alliance for Sexual Abuse Prevention and Treatment.

Gunnar, M. R. (2000). *Early adversity and the development of stress reactivity and regulation.* Bethesda, MD: National Institute of Mental Health.

Huntington's disease. (2002, June). Retrieved from http://aolsvc.health.webmd.aol.com/encyclopedia/article/4115.600.

Johns Hopkins Medical Institutions. (2002, January 14). Study examining inheritance patterns of panic disorder and manic depressive illness. *Science Daily.*

Kendall-Tackett, L. A. (2000, June). Physiological correlates of childhood abuse: Chronic hyperarousal in PTSD, depression and irritable bowel syndrome. *Child Abuse & Neglect.*

Learning disabilities: Decade of the brain. (2002). Washington, DC: National Institutes of Health.

Lisa, F. (2001, May 9). *Paying attention. Education Week,* 26–29.

Moyzis, R. (2002, January 8). A gene study linking a variant form of a gene to ADHD. Washington, DC: National Academy of Science.

Newborns are amazing: Hands on help for parents. (1998). Minnesota, MN: Meld.

Next frontier. (2002, June 24). *Newsweek,* 41.

Open your mind. (2002, May 25). *Economist,* 77–79.

Palmer, L. K, Frantz, C. E., Armsworth, M. W., & Swank, P. (1999). *Neuropsychological sequelae of chronically psychologically traumatized children: Specific finding in memory and higher cognitive functions, trauma and memory.* Thousand Oaks, CA: Sage.

Pantev, C. (2002, January 10). *Study of possible musical training on brain function in young and old.* Toronto, Canada: Rotman Research Institute.

Perry, B. D. (1992). *Neurodevelopment and the psychophysiology of trauma 1: Conceptual considerations for clinical work with maltreated children.* Houston, TX: Baylor College of Medicine.

Perry, B. D. (1998). *Traumatized children: How childhood trauma influences brain development.* Houston, TX: Baylor College of Medicine.

Rimland, B. (1998). *The autism explosion.* San Diego, CA: Autism Research Institute.

Schlaug, G. (2001, May). *Musical training during childhood may influence regional brain growth.* 53rd Annual Meeting of the American Academy of Neurology, Philadelphia.

Silver, J. A. (2000). *Integrating advances in infant research with child welfare policy and practice, protecting children.* Englewood, CO: American Humane Association.

Sohn, E. (2002, June 10). The hunger artists. *U.S. News & World Report,* 44.

Studies link child abuse to brain changes. (2002, May). *Children's Voice, 11,* 47.

Television can enhance children's intellectual development, study finds. (2001, September/October). Available from http://www.sciencedaily.com/releases/2001/09/010924061623.htm.

U.S. study finds brain undeveloped in premature infants. (2000, October 18). Available from http://www.cnn.com/2000/health/children/10/18/healthbirth.reut/.

Wade, N. (2002, June 18). Hunting for disease genes in Iceland's genealogies. *The New York Times,* D4.

Weinstein, J. D., & Weinstein, R. (2002, June 18). *Neuropsychological consequences of child neglect and their implication for social policy.* 13th National Conference on Child Abuse and Neglect. Retrieved from http://calib.com/nccanch/cbconference/resourcebook/72.cfm.

CHAPTER 3

21st-Century Health Problems in High-Risk Children and Youth

I Never Thought I'd Worry About Obesity in Kids!

Child welfare workers need to understand physical and mental health trends in children and youth. Many health issues in children are different than they were in the 1970s. For instance, workers did not think low levels of lead exposure were a significant health risk, and Asperger syndrome was not a familiar diagnosis.

Poverty plays a big role in how children grow and develop. According to Doug Vaughn, it is the largest barrier to a good beginning in life. Recent indicators reflect rising poverty, and in 2000, at least 16.2% of U.S. children lived in poverty. Sadly, children are 37% of the nation's poor.

Nationally, more than 60% of all families headed by nonparent relatives have low incomes. According to the Urban Institute, a nonpartisan research center, nearly half of these families had trouble buying enough food, and about 40% had trouble meeting their housing costs.

Some health problems are getting worse. For example, workers are seeing children with severe mental health problems and having to treat them at younger ages. Marie Sophie, a 30-year nursing veteran working on a children's psychiatric crisis unit remarked, "I see younger and more violent children than when I began working. And doctors are prescribing a lot more anti-psychotic medication." According to Sophie and other workers, children are also overdosing on aspirin substitutes, their own medications, and often their parents' prescription drugs when they attempt to harm themselves. The following are additional health trends affecting children and youth in the 21st century that worry child welfare advocates.

Poor Nutrition

Health care professionals are gravely concerned about what kids eat. Dr. Mulready, a family practitioner, reported that human bodies were not designed for the level of processed food being dumped into them. Processed foods, loaded with unhealthy fats, do not feed the brain and slow down the body. According to Mulready, whole grains, low-fat proteins, healthy fats such as olive oil, and fresh vegetables are essential. Unfortunately, bad food is more accessible and most familiar to kids in this fast-paced society.

Rising Obesity in Children and Youth

The number of seriously overweight and obese youth is increasing. Research shows that 60% of overweight children ages 5 to 10 already have at least one risk factor for heart disease, including elevated blood pressure and insulin levels.

Obesity can cause serious problems, including heart disease and Diabetes II, as well as inhibit social functioning. Experts believe this trend is largely due to a diet high in calories from fast foods and an inactive lifestyle, posing a new question to child welfare workers when they consider endangerment to children by caregivers (Patten, 2001). For example, what happens when a parent does not monitor a child's diet to the extent that the child is seriously impaired?

Exposure to Lead and Other Hazardous Substances

Researchers know that lead is the major hazardous substance now affecting children. In 1999, some 900,000 children between 1 and 5 had blood lead levels higher than the Centers for Disease Control and Prevention's (CDC's) level of concern. Research has shown that low levels of lead exposure once thought safe are dangerous. In 1994, the Consumer Product Safety Commission (CPSC) recalled 12 brands of crayons imported from China because they contained lead. CPSC also found that some imported mini-blinds contained lead and in 1996, identified various playground equipment with deteriorating lead containing paint chips and dust.

Lead can be found in water running through old plumbing as well as waste sites. Child welfare workers know that many of their clients live in older buildings and are not familiar with the fall-out from lead exposure. Some lead poisoning symptoms include learning disabilities, short attention span, stunted growth, aggressive behavior, and even death. Child advocates need to know that this not an easy condition to identify.

Other hazardous substances include PCBs, solvents, asbestos, radon, mold, pesticides, and air pollution. These materials can be found in the air, on playgrounds, in food, at schools and in homes. The following page lists questions that caseworkers and doctors should ask parents about children's possible exposure to toxic substances.

Lapsed Immunizations

Community health workers have growing concerns that many infants from poor homes are not completing their vaccination series. More than

---

Ask Parents These Questions About Exposure to Toxic Substances

Child advocates need to remind health workers to ask parents about exposure to toxic pollutants during examinations, or ask parents themselves and advocate in parents' behalf:

- Has your child been exposed to carbon monoxide from a faulty heating system? Learn about and teach parents how to look for faulty systems.

- Has your child played in an area later discovered to contain toxic waste?

- Has your child gotten ill only in his or her school building?

- Has your child been near a dry cleaners or laundry and exposed to radon?

- Have you ever gotten a report to see if there is arsenic in your water?

one-quarter of African American infants do not receive all their shots. Infants who are not up to date at 3 months are likely to be undervaccinated overall. A growing disparity also exists between infant immunization in poorer homes and higher income homes (Center for the Advancement of Health, 2001). Another role in child welfare work is investigating these gaps as they pertain to the safety and well-being of children.

Undiagnosed or Exposure to Hepatitis B and C

It is estimated that each year, approximately 20,000 infants are born to women infected with Hepatitis B (HBV), putting them at high risk for perinatal infection and chronic liver disease as adults. Fewer than half of these births are reported to state and county health departments. Child welfare workers are affected because children with HBV need intensive case management and supervision (Hepatitis Information Network, 1997).

Infants born to women with Hepatitis C can experience jaundice, abdominal pain, loss of appetite, nausea, and vomiting. This disease can lead to chronic liver disease later.

Eating Disorders

Eating disorders continue to be a problem. Of the people affected, 90% are adolescents and young adult women. Three types are anorexia nervosa—intentionally starving oneself, most often beginning at puberty; bulimia nervosa—obsessively consuming large amounts of food and then vomiting, abusing laxatives, taking enemas, or exercising; and binge eating—eating large amounts of food and not stopping until uncomfortably full, but not purging. Obesity is a natural outgrowth of binge eating, and in many depressed areas of the country, children are getting heavier. Eating disorders can damage vital organs and the respiratory system, cause anemia, rot teeth, and cause irregular menstrual periods, obesity, high cholesterol, and diabetes. Child welfare workers may become involved when children miss school, become depressed and socially isolated, or do not receiving adequate medical intervention by their caregivers ("Eating Disorders," 1999).

Undiagnosed or Pediatric and Adolescent Exposure to AIDS

AIDS is a chronic illness caused by infection by HIV. HIV is transmitted through exchange of bodily fluids, such as blood, semen, vaginal secretions, and breast milk. New treatments have helped hold back the progression of this disease, yet it continues to be a health concern. It is important to remember that health maintenance regimens are costly and can take a physical toll.

Of babies born to untreated mothers infected with HIV, 25% to 30% develop the infection themselves. In New York City in 1998, AIDS was the leading cause of death in Hispanic children 1 to 4 years old and the second leading cause of death in African American children the same age.

Adolescents are at risk to acquire HIV because of their impulsivity. Every day, one person younger than 25 dies of AIDS. Acquiring tattoos and body piercings is risky because youth may not know if they are being pierced with contaminated needles or instruments. Increased drug and alcohol use lowers inhibitions, and often, adolescents' magical thinking ("I won't get pregnant" or "Oral sex is not really sex") supercedes using protection ("Infants, Children," 1999). All of these behaviors place kids at risk and complicate the role of the child welfare worker due to confidentiality concerns.

Increased Reports of Attention-Deficit/Hyperactivity Disorder (ADHD)

The *Diagnostic and Statistical Manual for Mental Disorders* (4th ed.; American Psychiatric Association, 1994) estimates that 3% to 7% of children suffer from ADHD. It is diagnosed three times more often in boys than girls. ADHD is one of the more common neurobehavioral disorders of childhood and can continue into adulthood. Research points to brain conditions that contribute to this disorder. Three types of ADHD exist: predominately inattentive—easily distracted or forgets details of daily routines; predominately hyperactive/impulsive—excessive fidgeting and talking, difficulty with impulses; and predominately combined—symptoms of both types equally predominant. Some child advocates and parents feel that this disorder is being overly diagnosed, to the extent it is now becoming a child welfare issue (American Psychiatric Association, 1994).

Child welfare workers often have the challenge of identifying and referring children for evaluation and treatment of these disorders. Multiple problems within the child as well as the child's family can exacerbate their job. Some of the coexisting conditions include conduct, anxiety, depressive, or manic-depressive disorders. Meanwhile, children with ADHD can suffer socially as well as academically.

Increased Reports of Conduct Disorder and Oppositional Defiant Disorder

Child welfare workers frequently see children with these two disorders. More information about them has come to light in recent years. Many children in the juvenile justice or residential treatment systems suffer from a "persistent pattern of behavior in which the basic rights of others or major age-appropriate social norms are violated" (American Psychiatric Association, 1994). Although researchers have gained insight into the disorders, they continue to remain extremely difficult and persistent mental health problems.

Child welfare workers can intervene early if they know that irritable temperament, poor compliance, inattentiveness, and impulsive behavior in children as young as 2 can lead to conduct disorders later.

Violence can erupt in families when parents resort to extreme punishment in their attempts to control a child with one of these disorders. Negative patterns of communication can emerge, and child abuse can happen. Conduct disorder and oppositional defiant disorder often coexist with other mental health problems such as ADHD, depression, anxiety, and attachment disorder (American Psychiatric Association, 1994).

Problematic behaviors include oppositional, defiant behaviors and antisocial activities. Many violent children have a history of aggression toward people and animals, property destruction, lying and theft, and serious rule violations.

Increased Diagnosis of Post-Traumatic Stress Disorder (PTSD)

Children can be severely affected by earlier situations that caused them to experience terror. Understanding PTSD and its connection to various forms of violence is important for child welfare workers to understand. Researchers have discovered that the brain can be altered by even one terrifying experience, to the extent that it creates an anxious condition within the body. Long after a trauma has occurred, children can be triggered into fight or flight reactions, tricking them into physically or emotionally re-experiencing what appears to be the original event. PTSD is an anxiety disorder that represents a cluster of symptoms children acquire over time to fight against anxiety and depression. Their condition can lead to hyperarousal, aggressiveness, avoidance behaviors, reenactment, hypersensitivity, and a score of other problems.

Other conditions in anxious children include the inability to speak in their own behalf, exaggerated startle responses, a feeling of invisibility, as well as hypersensitivity about being misunderstood. The core issue for children with PTSD is seeking physical and emotional safety. Child welfare workers need to approach working with youth from that angle (Levy & Orlans, 1998).

Increased Recognition and Treatment of Attachment Disorder

Attachment disorder has been identified recently because it appears that more children are unable to form a healthy attachment or bond with their caregivers. Children with attachment disorder exhibit a variety of aggressive, antisocial behaviors. Stealing, lying, hoarding, inappropriate sexual behavior, chronic body tension, cruelty to animals, enuresis and encopresis, and a preoccupation with evil are some of the characteristics of this diagnosis.

A child will frequently also have conduct disorder and PTSD with attachment disorder. Children adopted from war-torn countries may have an attachment disorder, as well as children of drug abusing or mentally ill parents. The juvenile justice system often incarcerates children with this problem because they hurt other children. Long-term residential care is usually needed to treat their problem (Galant, 2002).

Autism

Autism is a disability that affects a child's ability to relate to other people. Autism was first identified in 1943. Until 10 years ago, it was thought that

Table 2
Drug Classifications and Their Use

Drug Classification	Medications	What Is Treated	May Help Treat	Comments
Stimulants	Dexedrine, Adderall, Ritalin, Concerta, Metadate, Focalin, Cylert	ADHD, narcolepsy	Conduct disorder	
Antidepressants	Prozac, Zoloft, Paxil, Celexa, Luvox, Effexor, Remeron, Tofranil, Pamelor, Norpramine, Elavil, Anafranil, Serzone, Desyrel**, Wellbutrin	Depression and anxiety disorders (generalized anxiety, social phobia, OCD, PTSD, panic disorder), bulimia nervosa	Conduct disorder, night terrors, sleepwalking	Tofranil indicated for enuresis and helpful in ADHD; Desyrel used for insomnia
Antipsychotics	Risperdal, Zyprexa, Seroquel, Geodon, Abilify, Clozaril, Haldol, Loxitane, Mellaril, Moban, Navane, Orap, Prolixin, Stelazine, Thorazine, Trilafon	Schizophrenia, other related psychotic disorders (disorganized thinking) and Tourette's disorder	Conduct behaviors associated with autism, mental retardation, violent behaviors	

	Medications	Indications		
Mood Stabilizers	Lithium carbonate, Tegretol, Depakote, Depakene, Zyprexa, Lamictal	Bipolar disorder or schizoaffective disorder	Given in adjunction with antidepressants as augmentation therapy for treatment resistant depression	May help in decreasing violent and severe aggressive behaviors associated with conduct disorder
Anxiolytics	Ativan, Klonopin, Xanax, Serax, Valium, Librium, Tranxene, Ambien, Vistaril, Buspar	Severe anxiety disorders except OCD	Note: All are sedative-hypnotics except Vistaril and Buspar	
Other medications	Antihistamines: Benadryl, Vistaril, Periactin Alpha 2 agonists: Catapres, Tenex Betablockers: Propanolol, Tenormin, Visken, Corgard Desmopressin spray	Insomnia and anxiety ADHD, Tourette's Anxiety, stage freight, aggressive and violent behaviors, PTSD, opioid withdrawal Nocturnal Enuresis	Poor appetite associated with stimulants Flashback--PTSD Tremors or restlessness associated with other medications	

Source: Eneida Gomez, MD.
Note: ADHD = attention deficit/hyperactivity disorder; PTSD = post-traumatic stress disorder; OCD = obsessive compulsive disorder. The physician may use a psychotropic medication at his or her discretion for other indications or behaviors not mentioned here.

there were about 5,000 children with this condition, however, doctors have recently identified many more children.

Autistic children may be rigid about their routines, overreact to certain triggers, and fixate on specific subjects. They may engage in repetitive movements, such as head banging or arm flapping. The condition is four times more common in boys than girls.

Asperger syndrome is a mild form of autism and is a condition in which verbal skills are generally quite good, but tone and facial expression are abnormal. Youth with Asperger syndrome have poor social skills due to their inability to read and transmit nonverbal cues accurately. They also have difficulty understanding how other people feel and they tend to become obsessed with one subject.

Pediatric crisis units are dealing with more autistic children when they become violent. Autism can socially isolate families and create excessive stress for all family members. To date, no cure for autism exists, and medications range from antidepressants to antipsychotics. Early detection is the key to helping these children. Sometimes autistic children are misdiagnosed with conduct disorder, causing additional problems, because interventions for the two are different.

Mood Disorders

Child welfare workers are seeing younger children with mood disorders. Depression is sometimes recognized, even in infants. More children are suffering from other mood disorders such as anxiety (seen in PTSD) and bipolar disorder, or manic-depression. Doctors have diagnosed bipolar disorder in addicted youth. It can co-occur with attention-deficit disorder (ADD), because both share symptoms such as impulsive behavior, poor judgment, and excessive activity. ADD is different because it can be identified before the age of 7. Table 2 shows various medications for mood disorders and what illnesses doctors use them to treat.

Understanding the Challenge

Child welfare workers seem to understand that many physical and mental problems affecting children are becoming more severe, but may continue to go undiagnosed. An estimated two-thirds of all young people with mental health problems are not getting the help they need. Part of the problem lies in the fact that culturally competent health services are not available in many communities. The challenge in helping kids and their families is in offering services that threaten them as little as possible.

Finding an ethical compass becomes our challenge as we navigate through complex health problems in fragmented and traumatized communities. Healthy markers along the way include accurately identifying problems, understanding clients' cultural norms, using wraparound services, and frequently checking to see if our interventions have been helpful. No one said it was easy, but making these connections can be extremely gratifying.

References

American Psychiatric Association. (1994). *Diagnostic and statistical manual of mental disorders* (4th ed., text rev.). Washington DC: Author.

Center for the Advancement of Health. (2001). Black and poor infants short-changed on immunizations. *Daily University Science News*. Available from http://unisc.com/stories/20012/042305.htm.

Eating disorders. (1999). Bethesda, MD: National Institute of Mental Health.

Galant, D. (2002). *Under the autism umbrella medical library.* Retrieved from http://webmd.aol.com/content/article/1665.53638.

Hepatitis Information Network. (1997). *Hepatitis B puts infants at risk.* Pointe Claire, Canada: Michael Betel.

Infants, children & HIV: Just the facts. (1999). Washington, DC: National Pediatric & HIV Resource Center.

Levy, M. T., & Orlans, M. (1998). *Attachment, trauma, and healing.* Washington, DC: CWLA Press.

Patten, P. (2001, January-February). Obesity in children: Should parents be concerned? *NPIN, Parent News.* Available from http://npin.org/pnews/2001/pnew101/int101f.html.

Toxic chemicals & health: Kids' health: In depth report. (1998). National Resources Defense Council. Available from http://www.nrdc.org/health/kids/ocar/chap3.asp.

Additional Resources

About children's environmental health. (2002). Children's Environmental Health Network. Available from http://www.cehn.org/cehn/aboutceh.html.

ADHD. (2002, February). Washington, DC: National Center on Birth Defects and Developmental Disabilities.

Brown, A. B. (n.d.). PTSD: A biological response gone awry? *NARSAD Research Newsletter*. Available from http://www.narsad.org/pub/win02ptsd.html.

Children who can't pay attention. (1999). American Academy of Child and Adolescent Psychiatry. Available from http://www.aacap.org/publications/factsfan/noattent.htm.

Children's and adolescents' mental health fact sheet. (1996). Washington, DC: U.S. Department of Health and Human Services.

Clarke, J. C. (1996, Winter). *Language development in children prenatally drug exposed: Considerations for assessment and intervention*. Berkeley, CA: University of California, Berkeley, School of Social Welfare.

Foster care national statistics. (2001, July). National Clearinghouse on Child Abuse and Neglect Information. Retrieved from http://www.calib.com/nccanch/pubs/factsheets/foster.ctm.

Hepatitis C fact sheet. (1998). Atlanta, GA: Centers for Disease Control and Prevention.

Important advances in stemming mother-to-child transmission of HIV. (2000). Atlanta, GA: Centers for Disease Control and Prevention.

Journal highlights: Effects of diet on children. (1998, January 21). Retrieved from http://www.edweek.org/cw/vol-17/19health.h17.

Key facts about children and families in crisis. (2002, June 17). Washington, DC: Children's Defense Fund.

Koplan, J. P. (1999, October 27). *Journal of the American Medical Association*.

McQueen, A. (2001, July). *Federal statistics released*. Washington, DC: National Insitute of Child Health and Human Services.

The movement to leave no child behind: Quality child care helps parents work and children learn, child care fact sheet. (2001). National Center for Education Statistics.

Pregnancy and drug use trends. (2001, October). Rockville, MD: National Institute on Drug Abuse.

Psychiatric medication for children and adolescents, facts for families. (1999, November). Washington, DC: American Academy of Child & Adolescent Psychiatry.

Sedlak, A. J., & Broadhurst, M. L. A. (1996, September). *Executive summary of the third national incidence study of child abuse and neglect*. Washington, DC: U.S. Department of Health and Human Services.

Shannon, M. W. (2000, March). Risk assessment of children exposed to environmental pollutants. *Journal of Toxicology, 38*(2), 201.

Teen pregnancy. (1999, June). Washington, DC: U.S. Department of Health and Human Services, Chronic Disease Prevention. Retrieved from http://www.edc.gov/needphp/teen.htm.

Tynan, D. W. (2002). *Conduct disorder.* Retrieved from http://www.emedicine.com/ped/top2793.htm.

CHAPTER 4

Parenting, Violence, and Substance Abuse Issues in High-Risk Children and Youth

My Clients Used to Run Away; Now, They Shoot People

Outreach workers stood beside a Chicago elementary school in spring 2002, offering consolation to frightened students after children from a rival elementary school attacked them with baseball bats and wooden planks. The police arrested the attackers, ages 10 to 14, for mob action, conjuring up images of what might be in store for child welfare workers in the 21st century.

Another incident the same year struck fear into the hearts of residential treatment workers. On February 7, 2002, eight youth ages 14 to 16, living at a residential treatment community in a town ironically named Pleasantville, attacked a lone night counselor. They beat her over the head with a cordless phone, chopped off her hair, doused her with rubbing alcohol, and set her on fire. The girls then threw her down a flight of stairs and poured bleach on the woman's raw flesh (Campo-Flores, 2002).

Increased violence among children and youth is just one of the serious issues confronting child welfare workers, and it is growing to frightening levels. All over America, workers are exposed to danger as they attempt to work amid gangs, guns, and explosive tempers. One agency director reported that the local police department advised her workers to wear flack jackets when they went to work.

Children, too, are in greater danger. In addition to their other problems, they are exposed to Internet dangers and drug violence. These conditions reflect the current state of our society. Thinking about them may make us wish for the less-complicated world before terrorists and school shootings. The terrifying World Trade Center and Pentagon tragedies of September 11, 2001, remind us that it is not always possible to shield children or ourselves from fear.

Those of us who worked in child welfare 30 years ago dealt with some of the same problems, but not the number of children. We also paid more attention to runaways and truant students. Now, children are more deeply affected by violence and substance abuse. Oddly, although juvenile crime is down, gun crime has risen (Meckler, 2002). Guns raise the lethality bar when it comes to children and youth.

Shetler, a long-time agency administrator, attributes some of the rise in reporting not only to population growth, but increased networking through cell phones and e-mail. "There are fewer secrets in families now that children, families, and friends are talking to one another through the use of these devices."

The Primary Issues

The primary issues posing the greatest threat to the health and well-being of children are mounting violence and gun use, substance abuse, and absent parenting. Added to the mix are technological advances such as the Internet, which contribute to the complex, overwhelming material thrown at children before they are emotionally or intellectually prepared to handle it.

Because of these issues, child welfare professionals and volunteers are coping with an overwhelming number of children are requiring foster care and protective service intervention. Many of them, such as Tony, have multiple problems.

Tony's Story

> Children's Protective Services became acquainted with Tony as a newborn when he was placed in foster care while his mother entered drug rehabilitation. He stayed with his foster family for nine months before moving back home with his mother and grandmother. Tony's mother went through a difficult time with a boyfriend, however, and began to use drugs again when he was 18 months old.

By then, his grandmother was noticing that Tony was not developing the way other babies develop. His motor skills seemed delayed. She mentioned her concern to his CPS worker, and after a wait, he was diagnosed with cerebral palsy.

By age 3, Tony's grandmother was having difficulty coping with his special needs. She could not lift or drive him to all his appointments. She and the CPS worker decided to place him with a foster family who worked with special-needs children.

Other children lived in the home, and because he had more physical challenges, he was teased by his foster siblings. By the time he entered school, he was stuttering and had moved to another foster home. In school, he was easily distracted and fell behind. Tony was placed in remedial classes. Over time, he grew more frustrated by his disability and began to explode in bursts of temper.

His behavior was given a quick ADHD diagnosis, and he began to take medication to help slow his reactions. He was not seen regularly by the busy child psychiatrist, however, and the psychiatrist did not evaluate his medication in a timely way.

At age 10, Tony began seeing a therapist, who helped him express himself more easily, but when the agency replaced his caseworker after six months, his therapy got dropped. By the time he was 12, he had made friends with drug dealers at school, and they introduced him to marijuana. Eventually, his drug use escalated, and he was sent to a group home after his foster family became exhausted with trying to deal with his problem.

At 15, Tony still has problems controlling his temper, and he openly admits that he feels confident when he uses drugs. Like most adolescents, he is waiting for the time he will be independent, so that "I can start my life and live it the way I want." He sees his mother between long absences. His grandmother died when he was 11. He still has not met his father.

Finding Safety from Violence

From insidious Internet pornography to overt terrorist aggression, violence is now intense and extremely unpredictable. Helping children feel psychologically as well as physically safe in an unsafe and constantly changing world is a daunting challenge, not only for child protection workers but for parents everywhere.

For instance, it is estimated that 1 in 12 high school students is threatened or injured with a weapon each year, and youth between the ages of 12 and 24 have the highest risk of being victims of violence. The American Academy of Pediatrics is clear about their position that exposure to violence, including television, movie, and video game viewing is a health risk to children.

Teenagers are two and a half times more likely than adults to be victims of violence. Although young children are especially vulnerable, older youth are at greater risk for homicide. Despite recent declines, the adolescent homicide rate is still about 10% higher than the average homicide rate for all Americans. Interestingly, youth who were violent in the last year are more likely to use alcohol and illicit drugs during the past month than those who were not violent ("NHSDA Report," 2002).

Police arrest more than 123,000 children for violent crimes each year, and gunshot wounds to children younger than 16 has increased 300% in major urban areas since 1986 ("1999 Violence Fact Sheet," 1999). The combination of drugs and guns has created a 21st-century cocktail for youth trauma. Vincent Schiraldi, Director of the Justice Policy Institute in Washington, DC, said, "This sad reality [rising juvenile gun crime], probably has more to do with gun availability than any quantifiable difference in today's youth population."

Children are traumatized by exposure to gun violence within their social network. Said one Boston teenager, "A couple of my friends have died from shootings. It's normal. I feel like it is so common that now you take it as it comes to you, and you just keep moving on, one step at a time" (Holstrom, 1996, p. 1).

Guns were certainly accessible to the young killers at Colorado and

Georgia high schools, although research shows that schools are still the safest place for children ("Youth Arrest Data," 1999). Sadly, more youth die from gunshot wounds than from all natural causes combined (Gaensbauer & Wamboldt, 2000).

Other countries pale in comparison to the United States with regard to gun violence. In 1996, criminals used handguns to murder 9,390 people in the United States, whereas in Canada, they killed 106. Our country is not considering its children by making firearms so accessible.

Is One Gender More Violent?

Male youth continue to be involved in most of the violence. Females, however, have set a course of their own. Although girls almost never use guns, their aggressive behavior has steadily increased. From 1990 to 1999, arrest rates for girls rose 57%. Dr. Prothrow-Stitch, a Harvard public health professor, stated, "It is becoming more of a norm for girls to respond violently to situations than it used to be" (as cited in Lazar, 2002).

Another serious form of aggression relates to date and domestic violence. Not surprisingly, violence against mothers by their intimate partners is a risk factor for child abuse. One in five girls has experienced physical or sexual violence from a dating partner (Stark & Flitcraft, 1991). Child welfare professionals also work with a growing number of boys and girls who sexually molest siblings or other youth.

How Do We Prepare to Work in Potentially Violent Settings?

In understanding the realities of work today, some helpful considerations when working in reportedly violent areas of the community are:

- Teaming is essential when entering potentially violent parts of town. If this is not possible, check in with a coworker at a designated hour.

- Carry a beeper or cell phone and know emergency numbers. Let people know where you are going and when you will return.

- Take time to get to know a neighborhood. It can make a world of difference when people get to know you. Having coffee with natural helpers such as neighborhood watch and housing association members builds trust and may assist you when you do investigations or look for a parent or child.

- Meet business owners who have a stake in the community. Bake cookies for a foster grandparent. Make attempts to learn a few phrases in the language of the community.

- Do not react aggressively until you have gathered all the information about a potentially dangerous situation.

- Know the cultural norms of the community where you work. For example, speaking to an elder on entering the area will demonstrate your respectfulness in some communities.

- If there is a need, wear clothing protection and running shoes.

- Be realistic about potential dangers. When working with people you know to be drugged or intoxicated, be extremely wary. They can be unpredictable and sometimes dangerous. Meet at well-lit public places or during daylight hours.

- If you feel unsafe, leave the area and let your supervisor know. Do not be timid about calling for police protection.

- Work with other trusted people in the community, such as ministers, coaches, or schoolteachers.

While child welfare workers continue to grapple with these issues, other types of violence have recently come to light. Three less conventional but increasing problems are Internet danger, media violence, and bullying or fighting among children and youth.

Internet Violence

In spring 2002, a married man strangled a 13-year-old Connecticut girl while he molested her in his car at a mall parking lot. Described as popular and outgoing, the sixth grader had met her killer in an Internet chatroom ("School Girl," 2002). Around the same time, citing Internet danger to children, the U.S. House of Representatives approved a wiretap measure to seek wiretaps for suspected sexual predators to help block physical meetings between adult molesters and children. In addition, child advocates are working toward eliminating Internet pornography readily accessible to children who surf the Web (Blom, 1998).

The Crimes Against Children Research Center (CCRC) at the University of New Hampshire studied this new trend in sexual abuse and concluded that compared with other ways that young people are sexually victimized,

Employers Have a Responsibility to Provide a Safe Workplace

Employers may be liable if they knew or should have known about safety risks that can harm employees. Regina Young, Attorney, gave the following advice on providing a safe workplace when a potential for violence exists:

- Building visitors should register and pass through a secured door and metal detectors.
- A workplace should provide adequate lighting indoors and in parking areas.
- Workers should carry beepers and have emergency response numbers.
- Partnering with other workers when entering potentially dangerous areas is part of ensuring worker safety.
- Emergency response buttons need to placed in potentially violent places at work.
- When possible, an organization must install and maintain locks, alarm systems, and security cameras.
- Offices and residential facilities should have peepholes and buzzers.
- Evening security guards who escort workers to cars are important in providing worker safety.
- Regular self-defense classes help workers understand their strengths and limitations.
- Providing adequate staff to cover client need is essential.
- Workers should immediately inform supervisors about a potentially dangerous workplace condition. If supervisors fail to respond, workers may pursue action by presenting their concerns in writing, keeping copies for themselves. When presenting a concern in writing, it is always good to request an answer within a reasonable time frame.

cases of actual liaisons or assaults originating on the Internet appear to be uncommon. Lack of good data, however, makes this a difficult topic to assess. Dr. David Finkelhor, CCRC Director, said that sexual offenses generally against young people are greatly underreported. The CCRC survey also showed that youth as well as adults are sexual predators on the Internet (Slavin, 2002).

Other dangers are brought about through the Internet. Online game playing is costing children a large chunk of their time at the expense of their daily lives. In online team games, kids form bonds with other players to the extent that peer pressure adds to online time as well as guilt when they log off. A young man in the Midwest shot himself after disengaging from a game site ("Online Game," 2002). He had spent months online isolating himself and becoming increasingly depressed. Mental health professionals receive calls from family members and online junkies who are worried about Internet addiction to the extent they neglect friends, family, school, and other responsibilities. Child welfare advocates need to know the problem is not going away.

The Internet is a way to make drug connections as well. An example is the legal sale of salvia extract, a hallucinogenic plant children and youth now abuse. To quote an advertised sales pitch from one the websites, "Our salvia is grown in [the] Oaxacan region of Mexico and we take orders from anywhere in the world (including Australia where the killjoys recently banned it)."

Media Violence

Children's television has changed dramatically since the days of "Leave It to Beaver." The average American child now watches 45 acts of violence on TV each day, most of which involve handguns. Studies of the effects of TV violence on children and teenagers have found that children may become desensitized to violence, gradually accept violence as a way to solve problems, and imitate the violence they observe on TV (Gaensbauer & Wamboldt, 2000). This numbing condition may also apply to video games, movie, and music. The Office of Juvenile Justice and Delinquency Prevention listed exposure to media violence as a risk factor affecting juvenile delinquency (Wingfield & Albert, 2001).

More than 3,500 research studies have examined the association between media violence and violent behavior; all but 18 have shown a positive relationship. Children learn by observing and trying out behavioral scripts. Consistent exposure to violent behavioral scripts can lead to increased hostility, anticipation of aggressive behavior from others, desensitization to others' pain and a higher likelihood of being violent.

Bullying and Fighting Among Kids

Mulvey (2001), Director of Law and Psychiatry in Pennsylvania, indicated that 37% of high school students were in fights in 2001, and 80% of those children engaged in bullying. Bullying appears to have played a role in adolescent shooters' killing their classmates. For instance, two teenagers who killed 1 teacher and 12 students and wounded 23 others at Columbine High School in Littleton, Colorado, had, over the years, been teased and called "faggots." Another student in Mississippi killed two students, wounded seven, and stabbed his mother to death after a girlfriend broke up with him, calling him pudgy and gay. Other school shooters had endured years of verbal abuse by classmates.

Bullying can traumatize children, making them depressed and anxious (Banks, 1997). When this physical or psychological intimidation repeatedly occurs, children can acquire PTSD symptoms.

Protecting Ourselves Is a Priority

Child welfare workers must be careful about their personal safety when they approach potentially violent children or family members. Demanding measures to safeguard them from exposure to violence at work are necessary. Often, they are alone when they get hurt by an aggressive child or caregiver and immediate help is unavailable. The residential child care worker who was set on fire in Connecticut was by herself the evening she was attacked.

Workers are also at risk of secondary traumatic stress, an anxious condition, because of exposure to violence through their clients. They have probably known a child or family member who has been seriously harmed or killed by a violent act. When workers experience stress due to empathy with clients' situations and do not have an opportunity to process it through discussion or relaxation, they can become anxious and depressed. The following page shows what workers can do to help prevent youth violence and keep themselves from being put at risk for secondary traumatic stress.

Substance Abuse: A Core Issue

In May 2002, 5-year-old Angie, traveling alone, arrived in New York City from Bogota, Columbia, wearing a smile and carrying a suitcase holding 1,042 grams of heroin. Police suspected that her mother, who had been deported to Colombia in 2000, had placed the drug in her daughter's bag. In front of her grandmother and aunt, the child was handed over to CPS and placed in foster care.

It is estimated that 500 to 600 teenagers are detained every year in smuggling cases. A federal investigation in Chicago discovered an alleged smuggling ring originating in Panama. Police arrested 35 people for "renting" infants to help smugglers import cocaine hidden in the babies' formula bottles (Smalley, 2002).

Child welfare workers are increasingly presented with the frightening fact that caregivers are using children more and more as drug trafficking mules. Transporting illicit drugs is another way children have been harmed by the rising substance abuse crisis in the 21st century.

A Staggering Problem

The alcohol and drug problem is staggering. A study by The National Center on Addiction and Substance Abuse at Columbia University (CASA, 1999) found that children of drug- and alcohol-abusing parents are the most vulnerable, endangered people in America.

The number of abused and neglected children more than doubled from 1988 to 1999 due to parental involvement in drugs and alcohol. Substance abuse causes or exacerbates 7 out of 10 cases of child abuse or neglect. Kids whose parents abuse drugs and alcohol are almost three times more likely to be abused and more than four times more likely to be neglected than children of parents who are not substance abusers. Children exposed in utero to illicit drugs are one to two times more likely to be abused or neglected (CASA, 1999).

The child welfare system is overwhelmed by the problem of drugs and alcohol in families. The number of helpers exceeds the current capacity to assist families. Substance abuse can be linked to the number of children in foster care, 568,000 as of September 1999, which doubled since 1986, causing a vast strain on the child welfare system and a shortage of intervention services to assist with this crisis.

What Child Advocates Can Do to Help Prevent Child and Youth Violence

Children who become violent may

- have a history of early aggression,

- have been exposed to violence at home,

- have experienced parental drug or alcohol abuse,

- engage in high-risk behavior,

- have experienced poverty and diminished economic opportunities,

- increasingly use drugs or alcohol,

- disclose detailed plans to commit such acts,

- announce threats or plans for hurting others,

- have access to weapons,

- have few trusting relationships with adults, and

- have experienced personal failure (Cloud, 1999).

Connect with a Child at Risk Using a Team Approach

- Engage teachers, birthparents, foster parents, extended family members, and counselors by sharing important facts about violence and planning ways to intervene with a potentially violent youth.

- Participate in ongoing risk assessments with the intervention team.

- Monitor children for transitions that can increase the likelihood of violence.

- Encourage peer support programs at school, faith communities, and other child-focused groups, such as Boy Scouts and Girl Scouts.

- When working with an aggressive child, always have back up. Never enter a potentially violent situation without a partner and notify support services.

- Remember to focus on resiliency strengths in children.

Drug Use and Pregnancy

AIDS was not around 30 years ago, and since then, an epidemic occurred and is now receding in this country. Intravenous drug use that infects prospective mothers with HIV remains a significant problem, however, especially for minority women and their babies. HIV transmission from mother to child during pregnancy, labor, delivery, and breastfeeding is responsible for 91% of all AIDS cases reported among U.S. children. In 1998, 80% of AIDS cases reported were among Hispanic and African American women.

In the absence of preventive drug treatment, an infected woman has a 25% to 30% chance of infecting her newborn. A total of 221,000 children are exposed to illicit substances during gestation each year, and more than 1 million to both illicit drugs and alcohol ("Facts About Families," 2000). A 1995 study analyzed data on about one-sixth of all HIV-exposed children and found that only about half received AZT treatment during pregnancy, delivery, and following birth. The problem lies in the fact that one-fourth of the mothers did not get prenatal care ("CDC Update," 1998). The good news is that perinatal transmission has dropped, and as a result of new treatments, HIV-positive children live longer lives.

Fetal alcohol syndrome (FAS) creates serious problems in children and is caused by women who drink heavily during pregnancy. Helping a child is

---

What Workers Say About Drug and Alcohol Abuse

CASA (1999) surveyed 915 child welfare professionals across the country about substance abuse and addiction:

- Of respondents, 80% thought that substance abuse causes or exacerbates most cases of child maltreatment.

- Of respondents, 90% thought alcohol alone or used with illegal or prescription drugs is the main abuse substance.

- Of illegal drugs, 48% cited crack cocaine as the most commonly abused, 20.5% cite marijuana, and 14.2% cite methamphetamine.

- More than 70% cited substance abuse as one of the top three reasons for the dramatic rise in child abuse since 1985.

more complicated when he or she suffers from central nervous system problems, growth retardation, and abnormal facial features, which are characteristics of FAS. Research estimates that between 1,300 and 8,000 children are born with FAS every year. Many more are born with alcohol-related neural-developmental disorder.

Serious conditions are present in children with these disorders ("Fetal alcohol syndrome," 2002). The most frequently diagnosed are ADD and ADHD, conduct disorder, alcohol or drug dependence, depression, and psychotic episodes. FAS causes children to become explosive and violent when they experience stress or frustration. Often, their ability to understand the motives of others has been compromised ("Living with FAS," 2002). Child welfare workers must understand the risks and be able to identify FAS so that children and families can be guided to appropriate resources.

Mothers addicted to crack cocaine can give birth to infants who are addicted as well. Babies often experience a characteristic withdrawal known as neonatal abstinence syndrome as a result of their mother's drug use. Research shows that cocaine can cause premature separation of the placenta from the womb and precipitate miscarriage or premature delivery. In addition, the babies have increased risk for sudden infant death syndrome (SIDS) and motor dysfunction. Infants may have a slightly smaller head circumference, raising concerns about brain growth.

Furthermore, children ages 2 to 5 who were born to methadone-maintained women seem to have an increased risk of learning disabilities and delayed motor, speech, and language development. Agencies need to create more intervention programs for alcohol- and drug-abusing mothers and their children.

Infants of addicted mothers also are at greater risk of abandonment. Between 1991 and 1998, the number of infants abandoned in hospitals increased by 46%, and the number of infants boarding in hospitals, or "boarder babies," beyond medical discharge increased by 38%. In 1998, 72% of these babies in hospitals were reportedly exposed to multiple drugs due to substance abuse by their mothers ("Facts About Families," 2000).

Researchers continue to increase their understanding of the harmful effects on children exposed to drugs in the womb. For example, children who are prenatally exposed have a high incidence of slow expressive language development, often accompanied by delays in receptive abilities, deficits in phonological or articulation skills, and deficits in impulse and socialization.

Mothers who smoke during pregnancy and following birth still worry health providers. For example, children who are breastfed by smoking mothers are at the greatest risk because chemicals are passed along in the breast milk. A new study suggested that mothers' cigarette smoking during or after pregnancy can increase the chances of an infant dying of SIDS by three times. Recent studies have also linked prenatal smoking to negative behavior in toddlers and smoking experimentation later by preadolescents ("Secondhand Smoke's," 2000).

Drug Choices

Child welfare advocates need to know about the types of drugs available to parents and children these days. One way to lose credibility with a young person is to demonstrate a lack of knowledge about the drug you are trying to persuade him or her from taking.

Different types of drugs have emerged in the past 30 years because many of them are now synthetic, or manmade. One of the more well-known and available in the 1970s was LSD. Things have changed. Although LSD continues to be abused, a highly toxic and addictive synthetic class of drugs called methamphetamine is now being taken throughout the country, and children are strongly affected by their parents' addiction to this drug.

Kids are increasingly caught in the middle of this drug explosion when their parents become manufacturers as well as addicts. Child welfare workers and law enforcement officers have come across some grisly scenes when they began their investigations at homes where "meth" is produced.

Kids and Drugs

Children and youth are opportunistic drug users. Generally, they abuse over-the-counter products such as glue, Tylenol, or cough medicine more than illegal substances. In the past 10 years, the number of children using inhalants has almost doubled. In 2000, more than 2 million youth ages 12 to 17 reported using inhalants at least once in their lifetime. As early as fourth grade, children begin to sniff, or "huff." Inhalants are accessible and deadly.

Older youth use high-potency "club drugs." They cause serious health problems, and in some cases, death. Used in combination with alcohol or other drugs, they are made more dangerous.

Drug-Endangered Children Teams

Teams of law enforcement officers, social workers, public health nurses, and district attorneys in several states are working together to remove children from homes in which methamphetamine is produced to safeguard them from further abuse and neglect. They are aware of the serious risks faced by children who are present at these sites. For example, in March 2002, Los Angeles County, California, sheriff's deputies found four children begging for food in their neighborhood. They were left alone with no food, water, or electricity. A methamphetamine laboratory was found in the family's garage. The children were being "home-schooled."

Parenting: A Core Issue

The majority of welfare workers surveyed for this book cited poor or absent parenting as a causal factor of children's problems. The abundance of abused and neglected children speaks to the fact that there are thousands of birthparents who have abdicated their responsibilities for various reasons. As of 1999, only 42% of children in foster care had plans of family reunification, leaving child welfare workers, foster parents, courts, adoptive parents, extended family, and residential workers to raise the other 58%.

Negligent caregivers contribute to the fact that many children are left alone and exposed to dangerous people or find companionship among marginal friends. Peer pressure can take over when the source of acceptance and guidance comes from other companions. Gangs are left to organize and direct the lives of thousands of youth. Troubled kids often remark that they are supported more by other gang members than by their birthfamilies.

Although parent drug and alcohol abuse contributes to abuse and neglect, mental illness in caregivers presents an additional challenge to child welfare workers. One worker reported that a mother with a bipolar disorder suddenly stopped taking her medication. The woman's decompensation posed a serious danger to her children. Unfortunately, child welfare professionals are not given notice when clients stop taking their medications. Parents place their children at great risk if they do not follow orders to take medication.

What You Should Know About Addictive Substances

Every child welfare worker should familiarize himself or herself with addictive substances available to children and parents. It is a lot to keep up with, but well worth knowing.

Tobacco Smoking and Smokeless Tobacco Use. Tobacco smoking and smokeless tobacco use is associated with poor health and other short-term health problems. It may also be a marker for underlying mental health issues, such as depression, among adolescents. Smoking causes damage to the respiratory system, addiction to nicotine, lung cancer, and cancers of the oral cavity, pharynx, larynx, and esophagus. It can cause damage to gums, may lead to loss of teeth, affects physical performance and is associated with the risk of other drug use.

Secondhand Smoke Exposure. Every year, exposure to secondhand smoke causes 150,000 to 300,000 lower respiratory tract infections, such as pneumonia and bronchitis, in U.S. infants and toddlers. Secondhand smoke increases the number of asthma attacks and the severity of asthma in 20% of the 2 to 5 million asthmatic children. Mothers who smoke at least 10 cigarettes a day can actually cause between 8,000 and 26,000 new cases of asthma among their children. A recent study suggests that infants are three times more likely to die of SIDS if their mothers smoke during and after pregnancy. Children exposed at home are more likely to have middle ear disease and reduced lung function.

Anabolic Steroids. Artificial hormones, steroids help in muscle and strength building. They also create aggressive behavior, grow breasts in men and body hair in women, cause acne and baldness, affect reproduction, and stunt growth.

Alcohol. Alcohol is a depressant that kills brain cells, impairs moods and judgment, and affects speech, drowsiness, and respiration. Alcohol causes convulsions, renal failure, aggressive behavior, hallucinations, slow body response, and alcohol poisoning. It also interacts negatively with medications.

Marijuana. Usually smoked but can be eaten, this plant contains hundreds of chemicals that are three times more potent than in past decades.

Effects of using marijuana include reduced short-term memory, difficulty concentrating while performing tasks, temporary increase in heart rate, paranoia and hallucinations, loss of physical and mental motivation, lung cancer, and a weakened immune system.

Khat (pronounced *cat*). Khat is banana-wrapped bundles of stems and buds. It originates in East Africa. Khat is chewed and creates euphoria, mild depression, and semicoma.

Over-the-Counter Drugs. These can be stimulants, such as weight loss pills, or depressants, such as cough medicines. These medications are taken excessively to achieve the desired affects by the abuser.

Prescription Drugs. Also known as speed, downers, bennies, nod, and uppers. Some of the abused forms include Tylenol with codeine, Valium, Ritalin, and painkillers, such as Percocet, Percodan, Tylox, Vicodin, and Oxycotin. Oxycotin is a brand name for the time-release tablet form of oxycondon, an opium derivative. When crushed or chewed, it gives a heroin-like rush, and it is highly addictive. Vicodin comes in tablets and combines a narcotic analgesic and cough reliever with a non-narcotic analgesic for the relief of moderate pain. Habit-forming, it can be fatal in overdose and cause nausea, sedation, vomiting, mood changes, constipation, lethargy, depression, and impaired mental and physical performance. Various prescription drugs can affect concentration and energy and cause insomnia, stomach problems, paranoia, hallucinations, and irrational thinking. Other effects can be increased heart rate and body tremors.

Inhalants. Inhalants include glue, nitrous oxide (Whippets), nail polish remover, spray paint, and rubber cement, also called Glue, Bullet, Locker Room, Rush, Texas Shoe Shine, and Bolt. Inhalants deprive the body and brain of oxygen and cause irregular heart rate. Sniffed, the mental and physical effects include sudden death; violent behavior; hallucinations; headaches; nausea; muscle weakness; drug tolerance; brain damage; loss of memory and reasoning; nosebleeds; liver, lung, and kidney problems; and hyperactive or sluggish behavior.

Club Drugs. Club drugs are synthetics that include MDMA (Ecstasy), GHB, Rohyphnol (Roofies), ketamine (Special K), PCP, methamphetamine, and LSD. They are commonly used at all night dance parties called "raves" or "trances." Foxy, also called Methoxy Foxy, is known as 5-MeO-DIPT. A hallucinogen, it comes in tablets and capsules causing diarrhea, nausea, severe anxiety, and a high or "buzzing" that can last 14 hours.

AMT, also called IT-290, is a hallucinogen that usually comes in a capsule with orange or off-white powder. It produces increased energy, empathy, visual patterns, nausea, headaches, vomiting, and jaw clenching. Ecstasy is a stimulant, psychedelic drug taken in tablet form, crushed and snorted, injected, or used as a suppository. It can cause permanent damage to the thought and memory sections of the brain. It can also cause nausea, faintness, fractured teeth, increased heart rate and blood pressure, and organ failure that leads to death.

GHB, a depressant available in odorless, colorless liquid form or as white powder material, is taken orally and often combined with alcohol. It has been used as a date rape drug and produces sexual arousal, amnesia, nausea, drowsiness, respiratory distress, dizziness, and seizures. Rohypnol is often sold in bubble packs and is prescribed as a sleeping pill in more than 50 countries outside the United States. It can also be ground into powder and snorted. A sedative/hypnotic depressant, it is used with other drugs such as alcohol, heroin, and cocaine. Another date rape drug, its withdrawal symptoms range from headache, muscle pain, and confusion to hallucinations, convulsions, and seizures.

PCP is ingested as tablets, capsules, or colored powders and snorted, smoked, or eaten. PCP produces feelings of invincibility and mind numbing that can often result in anger and rage. It can mimic primary symptoms of schizophrenia. Ketamine, or "special K," is a tranquilizer usually used on animals that comes in a liquid form consumed in drinks or added to smokable materials. The powder form can be added to drinks, smoked, dissolved, or injected, sometimes intramuscularly. Like Rohypnol and GHB, ketamine is a central nervous system depressant that can cause loss of muscle control, consciousness, and partial amnesia. It also produces distorted sight and sound perceptions, causing the user to feel disconnected and out of control. Respiratory depression, heart rate abnormalities, and a withdrawal syndrome are also associated with the drug.

Methamphetamine is a stimulant that speeds up the body and brain. Also called speed, meth, chalk, ice, crystal, glass, and crank, it comes as pills, powder, or clear chunky crystals. It can be swallowed, snorted, injected, or smoked. It causes aggressive feelings and behaviors, confusion, increased physical activity and heart rate, and permanent damage to blood vessels in the brain, leading to strokes. It causes loss of appetite, resulting in severe weight loss, and mental illness that mimics schizophrenia.

LSD is a hallucinogen, a mood-altering drug that affects perception. Odorless, colorless, and tasteless, LSD can be taken as tablets, capsules, or liquid. It is often added to absorbent paper and divided into small decorated squares. LSD causes depression, anxiety, fear, and panic. People also experience rapid mood swings, lack of muscle coordination, incoherent speech, and feelings of isolation.

Cocaine. This is a stimulant that comes from the leaves of the coca plant. The leaves contain about 2% of cocaine, which is removed by a chemical process. It is white and resembles crystalline powder. Crack cocaine looks like small (sometimes pink) rocks. It is injected, smoked, sniffed, or snorted. Smoking cocaine is called *freebasing*. Some users smoke "wollies," which are gutted cigars filled with marijuana, crack, or PCP. The effects of cocaine include angry, hostile, and anxious feelings; aggressive behavior; confusion; sleeplessness; loss of appetite; damage to blood vessels in the brain; convulsions and tremors; irregular heart rate and heart attack; and damage to nasal tissues and the septum when snorted, causing a runny nose, nosebleeds, and eventual destruction of the septum.

Heroin. Heroin is produced from morphine, which comes from a plant called the opium poppy and is processed into a bad-tasting powder that can be snorted or smoked. It can be white to dark brown. When it is dissolved and mixed with other liquids, it can be injected into the veins. Heroin is extremely addictive and causes nausea and vomiting, breathing problems, apathy, sleepiness, and extremes in mood.

Salvia Extract. This is an extract made by soaking *Salvia divinorum* leaves in a solvent to dissolve the *salvinorim*-A out of the leaves. It is smoked or taken orally and produces a 30-minute hallucinogenic high. Sold legally, usually on the Internet, has been known to create impaired judgment, aggressive behavior, and disorientation.

Mushrooms. Eaten raw, cooked, made into a drink, or dried, mushrooms are usually sold loose in bags or crushed into tablets. Effects are similar to LSD and include nausea, dizziness, vomiting, stomach pain, and hallucinations.

Parentless Children and Children of Single Parents

According to Dr. O'Gorman, Clinical Director for a statewide child welfare agency, many children have no family at all. O'Gorman feels that too many children are without any support, and their sense of loss and grief is severe. A problem is how to transition these young people from their placements to independent living when they turn 18. There just are not enough programs available to parentless children when they come of age. Finding independent housing is even more challenging when extenuating circumstances are involved, such as lack of economic support or mental and physical problems.

The percentage of children living with one parent increased from 20% in 1980 to 26% in 2000, and 50% of children live in a single-parent family at some point in childhood. Fatherlessness affects children's well-being as well. According to the National Practitioners Network for Fathers and Families ("About Fatherlessness," 1997), 90% of all homeless and runaway children are from fatherless homes. Fatherless children are twice as likely to drop out of school, and 63% of youth suicides live in fatherless homes.

Other Issues

Child welfare workers also report that children from middle-class homes are not getting their needs met in a different way. According to Jennifer, a nine-year veteran, "Middle-class parents are a huge part of the problem in today's society. Children get too much too fast. They don't have to work for things. The thing that children need most is time with caring adults." Many workers share the opinion that parents have too little time when both parents work.

High-quality child care is in short supply, and as Welfare to Work strategies challenge low-income caregivers to secure jobs, they must also find safe and affordable day care. It can be difficult when they work for minimum wage. Of children living in poverty in 1999, 31% had at least one parent working full-time year round. When money is scarce, children are more vulnerable to receiving poor day care supervision. Experts know that child care quality ranks close to family factors in how children develop ("Child Care Quality," 2000), and the following page lists some questions parents should ask about their day care centers.

Day Care

Accreditation in the National Association for the Education of Young Children is voluntary and only 10% of the nation's centers are accredited. Assessing day care can become part of a child advocate's job, along with delivering these helpful hints to parents. Guide them to ask the following questions when they consider their children's day care. The exercise may not create immediate changes but it could improve parent awareness:

- Does the day care have national accreditation?
- What is the staff-child ratio?
- How do children spend their day?
- How are children disciplined?
- Are parents free to visit anytime?
- What type of activities do they do to stimulate the brain and motor skills?
- How long has the day care been in operation?
- What experience and credentials do the staff have?
- What is the average teacher salary?
- How large are the classes?

Child Welfare Workers Need to Advocate for Children and Parents

Complex problems of the 21st century place workers in the precarious position of going the extra mile for struggling parents as well as children. As child advocates, we know there are usually many variables affecting any case. How we handle these complexities and build relationships keeps our personal integrity intact. The second section of this book discusses strategies and interventions to build professionalism and maintain a healthy perspective as it relates to child welfare work.

References

1999 violence fact sheet. (1999). American Academy of Child and Adolescent Psychiatry. Available from http://www.aacap.org/info-families/national-facts/99violfctsh.htm.

About fatherlessness. (1997). Washington, DC: National Practitioners Network for Fathers and Families.

Banks, R. (1997, April). Bullying in schools. *ERIC Digest*, University of Illinois.

Blom, E. (1998, October 11). Danger online: Child abusers exploit new opportunities via Internet. *Maine Telegram*.

Campo-Flores, A. (2002, February 25). Nightmare in Pleasantville. *Newsweek, 25*.

CDC update: Status of perinatal HIV prevention. (1998, May). Rockville, MD: Centers for Disease Control and Prevention.

Child care quality: An overview for parents. (2000, December). Champaign, IL: University of Illinois.

Cloud, J. (1999, May 31). Just a routine school shooting. *Time Magazine*, 34–42.

Facts about families, HIV/AIDS, & perinatal substance exposure. (2000). Available from http://socrates.berkekey.edu/~aiarc.

Fetal alcohol syndrome. (2002, May). Available from http://cdc.gov/ncbddd/fas..

Gaensbauer, T., & Wamboldt, M. (2000). *Proposal for CPS and CCAPS statement regarding gun violence*. Available from http://www.aacap.org/info-families/nationalfacts/cogunviol.htm.

Holstrom, D. (1996). Out of harm's way: Protecting children from violence—Part I. *Christian Science Monitor*, 1.

Lazar, K. (2002, March 11). Fighting like a girl: Female adolescents catching up to boys in aggressive behavior. *Boston Herald*. Available from http://www.bostonherald.com/news/local-regional/figh03112000.htm.

Living with FAS. (2002, March). Available from http://cdc.gov/ncbddd/fas/ fassc.htm.

Meckler, L. (2002, May 22). Child well-being on upswing in U.S. *Portsmouth Herald*, 1.

Mulvey, E. (2001, October). The inherent limits of predicting school violence. *American Psychologist, 56,* 797–802.

NHSDA report: Inhalant use among youths. (2002, March). Washington, DC: Substance Abuse and Mental Health Services Administration.

NHSDA report: Youth violence linked to substance use. (2002, March 5). Washington, DC: Office of Applied Studies, Substance Abuse and Mental Health Services Administration.

No safe haven: Children of substance abusing parents. (1999). New York: National Center on Addiction and Substance Abuse, Columbia University.

Online game killed son, anguished mom says. (2002, May 29). *Times Union*, A16.

School girl, 13, found slain; Chat room partner a suspect. (2002, May 22). *Times Union*, A5.

Secondhand smoke's effect on children. (2000). Atlanta, GA: Centers for Disease Control and Prevention.

Slavin, P. (2002). How safe are our children on the Internet? *Children's Voice, 11*(1), 24–28.

Smalley, S. (2002, May 6). The youngest mule. *Newsweek*, 48.

Stark, E., & Flitcraft, A. (1991). Spouse abuse. In Roseberg & Fenley (Eds.), *Violence in America*. Oxford University Press.

Wingfield, K., & Albert, R. (2001). Breaking the link between child maltreatment and juvenile delinquency, *Children's Voice, 10*(2), 89, 12.

Youth arrest data for 1999. (1999). Washington, DC: Office of Juvenile Justice and Delinquency Prevention.

Additional Resources

Alcohol. (2001). Washington, DC: National Clearinghouse for Alcohol and Drug Information, Substance Abuse and Mental Health Services Administration.

Alcohol, other drugs and child welfare. (2001). Washington, DC: Child Welfare League of America.

Alexander, A. (1999, May 30). Kids' troubles multiply. *Knight-Ridder Newspapers*, 1.

Atlanta meeting launches state fatherhood leadership conference. (2002, Winter). *Practitioner, 3*(2).

Child only welfare cases up as hardship and hunger grow. (2002, August 14). *The New York Times*, 1.

Children at risk—Bulletin. (2002, September 11). *Champions for Children Electronic Network*.

Club drugs. (2002, May). Available from http://www.clubdrugs.org.

Community alert bulletin: Methamphetamine. (1998, October). Rockville, MD: National Institute on Drug Abuse.

DASIS report: Drug and alcohol treatment in juvenile correctional facilities: Highlights. (2002). Washington, DC: Substance Abuse and Mental Health Services Administration.

Drug abuse and pregnancy. (1989, June). Rockville, MD: National Institute on Drug Abuse.

Drug facts. (2002). Washington, DC: Office of National Drug Control Policy.

Fact sheet. (2002, February). Washington, DC: Children's Defense Fund.

Fact sheet on Rohypnol. (1995, June). Available from http://www.health.org/non-govpubs/rohypnol.

Facts about MDMA (Ecstasy). (1999). *NIDA Notes, 14*(4).

Facts about violence among youth and violence in schools. (2001, March). Atlanta, GA: National Center for Injury Prevention and Control.

Facts about youth violence. (2002, May). Rockville, MD: National Center for Injury Prevention & Control.

Facts and myths about violence among youth and violence in schools. (2002, February). Atlanta, GA: Centers for Disease Control and Prevention.

Facts and myths about youth violence. (1999, March). *Youth Violence & Suicide Prevention*.

Facts on youth smoking, health, and performance. (2000, November). Atlanta, GA: Centers for Disease Control and Prevention.

Firearm facts. (2001, January). Available from http://www.bradycampaign.org/.

Frequently asked questions on child abuse and neglect. (2001, July). Washington, DC: National Clearinghouse on Child Abuse and Neglect Information.

Garland, S. (2002, March). The latest findings on day care. *Parents' Magazine*, 107–112.

Getting straight, the facts about drugs: A drug prevention book. (2001). Washington, DC: U.S. Department of Justice Drug Enforcement Administration.

GHB. (1998). Washington, DC: National Clearinghouse for Alcohol and Drug Information.

High school and youth trends. (2001, December). Rockville, MD: National Institute on Drug Abuse.

Inhalants. (2001, June). Washington, DC: Executive Office of the President.

Media violence. (2001, November). *American Academy of Pediatrics Committee on Public Education, 108*(15), 1222.

Methamphetamine abuse alert. (1999, March). Rockville, MD: National Institute on Drug Abuse.

Nicotine: Mind over matter teacher's guide. (2002). Rockville, MD: National Institute on Drug Abuse.

OxyContin facts. (2000). Boston: OxyContin Addiction Help.

PCP. Drugs and the brain. (1999). Atlanta, GA: National Families in Action.

Salvia divinorum: The legal high our politicians forgot to ban. (2002, February 25). Available from http://potseeds.co.uk/salvia.

School violence prevention. A Report of the Surgeon General. (1999). Available from http://www.mentalhealth.org/schoolviolence/.

Smalley, S. (2003, February 3). The perfect crime. *Newsweek*, 52.

Status of perinatal HIV prevention declines: U.S. declines continue. (1999, November). Atlanta, GA: Centers for Disease Control and Prevention.

Suicide: Cost to the nation. (2002). Washington, DC: Substance Abuse and Mental Health Services Administration.

Suicide in the United States. (2002, May). Atlanta, GA: Centers for Disease Control and Prevention.

Vicodin. (2002, January 24). Available from http://www.streetdrugs.org/vicodin.htm.

Warning signs: Violence to self. (2000). Available from http://helping.apa.org/warningsigns/index.html.

When kids kill. NISE Project. (2002). Available from http://whyfiles.org/065school-violence/1.html.

Youth violence in America. (2000). Atlanta, GA: National Center for Injury Prevention & Control.

Youth who carry guns: NHSDA report. (2001, September). Washington, DC: Substance Abuse and Mental Health Services Administration.

PART II

21st-Century Strategies

The fishermen know that the sea is dangerous and the storm terrible, but they have never found these dangers sufficient reason for remaining ashore.
—*Vincent van Gogh*

CHAPTER 5

Character Underlies Worker Accountability in the 21st Century

What Does Character Have to Do with Accountability?

> In my records, there is a period where I was unaccounted for myself. There were times when I didn't even have a caseworker. No one knew or cared who or where I was. The problem has always existed.
>
> —*Ashley, a veteran of 14 foster homes*

Due to human service agencies' need to justify financial support, child welfare accountability has been linked recently more to evaluation and outcome measures than personal character. Evidence-based research is a requirement written into every grant proposal to justify new initiatives, and outcome measures must justify program renewals. Consequently, human character discussion as it pertains to accountability has become somewhat overshadowed by the race for dollars.

Job accountability in child welfare is not simple. Terrific workers can find themselves caught between a rock and a hard place as they attempt to do their job and deal with increasing funding constraints and huge caseloads. "The workers are overwhelmed, under-trained and under-compensated," remarked one state representative in Florida. He was referring to the fact that workers' caseloads in Florida are excessively high, while the Child Welfare League of America recommends no more than 17 cases per worker (Canedy, 2002).

Current worker conditions make it extremely difficult to fulfill the child welfare vision set forth by leaders from around the country. Many workers may not be provided with enough support, and those who practice poor judgment or lazy professional behavior contribute to the problem.

For example, a caseload of 50 children and her late-term pregnancy could have influenced a child protection worker in Florida when she neglected to follow up on a home visit. Her intervention might have saved the life of a 2-year-old later killed by his babysitter. When the caseworker lied about seeing him, however, she clearly demonstrated a severe lapse in character (Padgett, 2002). Other lapses accounted for the dismissal of three other Department of Children and Family workers in Orlando when they also falsified their records ("DCF to Dismiss," 2002).

Feeling overwhelmed on the job does not justify unethical behavior. Although child welfare accountability includes many things, such as accurate documentation, supportive supervision, and adequate funding, personal character is most important.

Accountability and Right Character

In ancient Greece, the word *character* meant mask. One aspect of character is knowing our clients well enough to adopt the appropriate mask. Demonstrating character means that we adapt our masks to the needs of each child, so our job may include wearing many masks.

The Greeks knew that it was best to understand people through their qualities. They drew character assessment from observation, so deciding a child's residential status without first observing his or her meaningful relationships is not being accountable as it pertains to child welfare. Workers can make serious mistakes when they do not take the time to observe clients to assess a situation.

We demonstrate character when we adopt the appropriate mask based on the child's needs. Donning different masks does not mean we are phony or insincere. It means that workers have the capacity to discriminate between clients' needs and their own. For example, workers do not impose their large vocabularies on less-educated people or expect clients to change their cultural touchstones.

Not all character masks use language. One of the most effective masks is silent, positive role modeling. Other masks include humor, wisdom, nurturance, protection, and so forth.

Wearing only one mask in child welfare work can create rigid behavior and narrow one's ability to help children. It is simply too much weight for us to carry. Virginia Satir, a well-known family therapist, used to say, "There is a tyranny in only one right way." She intuitively knew that children's brains do not develop well with one-dimensional direction.

Using Inquiry

Furthermore, using inquiry in assessing clients' needs keeps workers grounded, because truth is eventually revealed through investigation. For instance, when a worker scratches the surface, she can discover that perhaps a reason why one teenager gets along at her new foster home has more to with being closer to her siblings and less about the worker's social work skills. Right character demands that we probe more deeply.

Without inquiry, we can set unrealistic goals for our clients as well. It is normal for new workers to adopt a naive goal that includes getting children away from bad situations into good situations, while connecting them with the right services to accomplish a clear and finished outcome. Assuming an outcome before taking time to inquire reflects poor workmanship and does not allow for planning more than one outcome.

Even when we ask the right questions, many cases can be messy, not to mention extremely ambiguous. For example, children removed from their homes still remember their birthparents, no matter how much their circumstances may have improved. Birthparents may not be more appropriate caregivers than adoptive parents. Poverty does not necessarily mean neglect. Accountability as it relates to character means we strive through inquiry to attain our goals, not that we always attain them perfectly.

In addition, practicing right character requires that we respond to our souls' desire to live authentically. Right character keeps us true to ourselves. We may recall people from our past who did not bow to pressure. They refused to compromise their values and demonstrated that a lone voice in objection among 10 in consensus can accomplish miracles.

Character, as it relates to child welfare accountability, also pushes us to examine exaggerated self-perceptions. If not careful, workers can fall into the trap of believing their actions are above reproach and begin to acquire hubris, the Greek word for pride.

When workers ignore their pride, however, they may burn out by expecting too much of themselves. Working exhausting hours, promising more

---

Confidentiality and Information Security

Confidentiality is a serious accountability issue in child welfare and includes anything that identifies a person as a client. Protecting client confidentiality is an example of how character is expressed. Here are some helpful tips:

- Interviews and phone calls should take place in areas where conversations can not be overheard.
- Cell phones are not considered confidential because they can be scanned electronically.
- Agency phone lines should not be answered in a manner that would compromise client confidentiality.
- Do not put identifying information on the outside of folders.
- Consent must always be in writing and explained, with agreement reached on understanding the content.
- Lock briefcases when handling files.
- Develop procedures within your agency for reporting breaches of security and confidentiality.
- Make consent forms specific and clear to each type of consent asked for.
- Information must be logged out of the secured area prior to leaving and logged back in at the end of a business day.

---

than they can produce, and idealizing their professional persona can eventually affect job performance.

The Opposite of Right Character

So what is the opposite of right character? According to Hillman (1999), author of *The Force of Character*, a person with "bad character would refer to a person with little insight....[This] is simply one who does not imagine who he is—in short an innocent. Innocence has no guiding governance but

ignorance and denial." The Greek philosopher Socrates considered ignorance to be like an arrow missing its target. If we believe that we are "walking a perfect path," we may become inflexible and perhaps miss the mark
when it comes to helping children and families. Adopting a perfect path can
be potentially dangerous to kids, similar to wearing only one mask.

When we play out our ignorance and miss our mark, we need to be willing to change. Self-judgment is not helpful, but self-responsibility is. If we
are open to learning from our hubris experiences, we can transform ourselves into better human beings.

Rodney Cook, Chairperson for the Coalition for Juvenile Justice, discussed his transformation from ignorance:

> *Many years ago, I ran a treatment program for youth in*
> *Oregon. There were a number of ways to punish kids if*
> *they acted up, but the method I believed to be most effec-*
> *tive was locking them up for a couple of days. "This will*
> *teach you a lesson," I assured them. I was displeased when*
> *the detention reform movement found its way to Oregon.*
> *It meant I had to learn new ways to deal with the kids who*
> *misbehaved....[Now, I know that] this trend of locking kids*
> *up is a serious step that has serious and harmful repercus-*
> *sions. Improper detention does not increase community*
> *safety and is a detriment to the kids we are seeking to*
> *help....As I reflect on those years I spent at the treatment*
> *center in Oregon, I thought sending kids to detention was*
> *in their best long-term interest. All things considered, it*
> *appears that I'm the one who has "learned a lesson."*

Right character means workers are obligated to examine their attitudes
and behaviors, admirably demonstrated by Mr. Cook. Sadly, many times in
the past, accountability was defined by imposed morale values, not inquiry.
Removing Native American children from their homes and placing them in
boarding schools was an ignorant act by the U.S. government and a sad
remainder that when people impose external morale virtues before having
sufficient understanding, they can go astray. If workers are unable to examine personal ignorance, they blunder into sensitive situations and preemp-
tively pass judgment.

In the following, Sabrina and Bobbie discuss their journeys through the
child welfare system, allowing us the opportunity to consider how their

guardians' characters played a role in their young lives. Their stories reflect varying degrees of child welfare intervention. You may consider how you would have handled their situations differently.

Sabrina's Story

Sabrina turned 18 last May. She sits in her chair, back straight, hair neatly groomed and makeup applied perfectly to her pretty face. She begins to tell her story, eyes cutting back and forth as she checks to see if her listener is paying attention.

Sabrina explains that her mother is an emotionally fragile person who had difficulty taking care of herself, let alone Sabrina, her 16- year-old brother, and her 14-year-old sister. Frequent moves and being cast in the role of parent proved overwhelming for Sabrina. At 15, she told her caseworker that she and her siblings could not live with their mom any longer. Her dad was in jail. She says, "It wasn't the easiest thing to do and I've felt like my mom blames me, even though we still talk."

She liked the judge and her guardian ad litem. "They listened to us. The judge even asked us into his office and he took off his black robe and sat in regular clothes so it would be more comfortable." At that hearing, he ordered Sabrina and her siblings to be placed in foster care. They were sent to live in different places for a number of reasons.

Three years, three caseworkers, and two foster homes later, Sabrina now lives in her own apartment through an independent-living program. She reports that although she had some positive experiences, she also had some disappointing ones. Her first foster family had their license revoked when it was discovered they hoarded money earmarked for the kids, housed strangers, and failed to provide clean living conditions. "The house was filthy!" reports Sabrina. "I was picking up cockroaches daily." She also stated that her foster family did not speak English very well and never sat down together for meals. There were three other girls in foster care living with her. Alone time with her foster parents was nonexistent, and they were frequently verbally abusive.

Finally, after much complaining from all four teenagers, one caseworker investigated. The foster parents were ousted from the foster care system. Sabrina felt disillusioned and betrayed. Her original hope when she asked the state to intervene was to live in a safe and nurturing home. Clearly, this had not happened.

Her next foster care setting was in the country, and two women shared foster parenting responsibilities. This home was easier, and she liked the fact that everyone sat down for meals. But she was getting close to getting out on her own and felt that they did not understand her need to be independent. Hadn't she practically raised herself already?

Sabrina currently attends junior college and works part-time in a dental office. She has goals. But her experiences remain vivid. When asked about her caseworkers, she shares this observation:

> My first caseworker came once a month, stayed for one hour, took notes, and left. It was really hard to reach her. My second caseworker was overwhelmed and told me so. She always sided with my foster parents and they didn't always tell the truth. Caseworkers need to know that there are some bad foster parents who are in it for the money. But she didn't want to listen to anything I had to say. I like my caseworker now because she's young and focused. She always returns my calls, and I have a good relationship with her.

Sabrina is a resilient young woman who survived some pretty tough situations. When asked if she had been in therapy, she said that a visiting counselor came to the foster home two times, but it was her decision not to continue. "It was helpful for me to draw my family tree and all that, but I'm sure things are going to get a lot better and don't think I've been affected by everything that's happened anyway.

Bobbie's Story

"When I was 4 years old, I came into the system," reports Bobbie, a dark-haired 20-year-old with a ready smile. "I was living with my grandmother when she developed cancer and died. I remember my aunt taking her to the hospital for the last time but dying in a car accident on the way home after dropping grandma off."

> Since my mom was selling her body for drugs, my dad wasn't around, and my grandfather was an alcoholic, I was placed with my sister. Angela and I were placed in a children's home for a little while until I was sent to live with my dad's sister. When I was there, my mom would

call us or come by and feed us these lies, and one time pulled a knife on my aunt. After that, I was moved to a foster home. I was 5 or 6. I was there a little while and then sent to live with my dad's brother in Kansas. I was sexually molested by my older cousins there until I was around 9. I told my aunt. I remember I said, "There are bad things happening to me," but she didn't believe me. I was smart though. I called my caseworker and was sent back to this state and put in another foster home. But it wasn't very good.

My sister and I went to live with older foster parents for about two years. This was a good home. They were a good family, but they thought they would not be able to adopt us because of their age. So we moved to another place and the people adopted us. But our adopted father was abusive and called us names like, "You're stupid!" After two and a half years, they decided they didn't want us! So Angela and I were put in a group home for about 18 months.

My sister started running away and having sex. I told her, "You're becoming just like our mother." I felt like my sister was ruining my life. And the staff at the group home were so rude. They didn't care about how we felt. Some were nice, but we were left out of lots of things just by living there.

Even when we were put in another home, it didn't last because my sister wasn't allowing people to help. After that, my sister and I were separated, and I was placed in a home at around 16. I was with a single woman who worked as a homebound therapist. We moved to Kansas when she got a new job. I liked her, 'cause she had been my caseworker at one point. We used to go shopping and stuff.

But then she met this guy online, and they started dating. I felt left out. This guy would tell her things about me on the side, and he had a bad past. I became alienated from them, and finally my foster mom told me that she loved him more than she loved me. I was suicidal by then and tried several times to commit suicide.

Bobbie pauses a moment as she points to the scars on her wrists and arms.

I asked my foster mom, "All I want to know is if I'm part of your family." She told me to go ahead and kill myself. I ended up moving back here after they found my suicide notes that were written with my blood. I was put in the hospital for four weeks.

People think I was trying to get attention with all those suicide attempts. I just wanted help. After that experience I went to live with a new foster mom and she's been great. She's my role model.

People have used me in many ways, and it's hard for me to trust. One of my foster mothers left me for a week, home alone with two illegal aliens and her kids. I was scared. Another foster mom didn't have a car. How can you have children and not be able to drive them places?

The one thing I don't like about the system is the lack of confidentiality. Everyone knows your business. It's like, "Oh, there's Bobbie, she attempted suicide." But I like my caseworker now. She's been consistent. If I just want to hang out, she's there for me. She's taught some good class-es on how to cook and stuff. She's energetic, funny and easy-going.

Bobbie sometimes talks to her birthfather. It is hard, she says, because he is always drinking. She seems resigned to the fact that both parents were not around. Until now, she has talked about her life in a matter-of-fact way, but she brightens when she describes her current situation.

My new foster mom said, "Go for it." And helped me find my first apartment. I'm in this independent-living pro-gram now and I also mentor other people. I have my own two-bedroom, two-bath apartment, and I go to school and work. I want to be a social worker or psychologist. It's a good situation.

Her enthusiasm fades as she continues:

> But it's kind of scary to live by myself. Every night before
> I go to bed, I call my foster mom because I'm afraid of the
> dark. You know? I'm still afraid of the dark.

Sabrina and Bobbie are survivors. They have a lot to teach us about worker accountability. Their overriding message is, "Don't show up if you can't focus on us." We may forget that our young clients need to be re-parented. They ask us to return their calls, listen to their complaints, be fair and enthusiastic, and role model adult behavior. Although they may reject attempts to be nurturing, they are secretly appreciative. They are not that different from other kids. They want to associate their caseworkers with warmth, acceptance, and positive perception.

Work can take on greater meaning when we ask ourselves, "How would I treat these children differently if they were my own?" We may be surprised by the response, because although we may go the extra mile for our birthchildren, we may not work as hard for children under our protective supervision. After asking ourselves the same question, however, we may realize that we are unnecessarily harsh with our own children while making allowances for supervised youngsters.

Becoming Unstuck

Being accountable on the job means examining how one becomes stuck making the same character mistakes. For example, sometimes workers postpone home visits because they want to avoid speaking to frustrated or angry clients or passing on bad news. Consequently, these important appointments are placed at the bottom of their to-do lists because the workers' have difficulty dealing with emotions.

Other times, workers may ignore other team members because they feel resentment. When they isolate themselves or practice avoidance, they lose sight of the goal to help children. Some workers may assume an attitude of "I have to do it myself because it'll never get done." Or, "Forget about telling her anything. She doesn't understand." *Unless we handle avoidance issues, we will not be fully accountable to our young clients, their families, or coworkers.*

Workers can examine avoidance habits by acknowledging that avoidance is one way to protect themselves from feeling vulnerable. When we are around strong emotions, personal memories can be touched. Often these memories are associated with painful experiences.

If workers become accustomed to the idea that uncomfortable feelings are like passing clouds and that someone's anger is seldom about them, they can slowly become more detached and less stuck when strong emotions are involved. Detachment is not the same as indifference; it is simply a way to see oneself as an observer rather than a victim.

When workers think they have learned everything about child welfare, they can become unstuck by taking a new class or being around excited and enthusiastic new workers. Plenty of people believe that experience means wisdom, but a person can be as ignorant at age 50 as age 20.

Another way worker accountability can be derailed is when workers demonstrate what the Buddhists call "foolish compassion." Foolish compassion happens when workers view clients from a certain perspective. If they see clients through pity or adopt "professional warmth," they see themselves as the helpers. This can also mean viewing clients as helpless. Remembering personal instances when someone saw us through that lens can trigger a wake-up call. True compassion does not set us apart from others—it directs us to stand parallel with them.

One other way to become unstuck is to consider the advice of our young clients. They have a lot to offer in the way of teaching experiences.

Children's Accountability Advice to Child Welfare Workers

- Please do not assume that every foster parent has a child's best interests in mind. Listen to the child if he or she tells you something is wrong.

- Please understand that it is really hard to move from place to place because each house has its own smell and way of doing things.

- Living with people from another culture can be extra hard, especially when they speak a different language.

- Check from time to time to see if foster parents are asking their kids to pay for basic necessities, like toothpaste and shampoo, out of their allowances.

- Please try to put yourself in our shoes and understand why we get upset.
- Please do not come for an hour and write notes when we are talking. We like it when you do something with us so we get to know you.
- Please remember that most of us want a family life that includes stability and nurturing.
- Please do not use information against us after we have told you something in confidence.
- Please do not complain about us to your coworkers.
- Let us write our version of what has happened to us and keep that in our files along with all the other information.
- We like it when you show an interest and call us back right away.
- We like it when you laugh and give us compliments.
- We want you to introduce us to our new caseworker if you are leaving. Give us time to get used to the idea. It is okay if you let us know how you are doing from time to time.
- Some of us do not want to live with our birthfamilies, but we do want to stay in touch.
- Please don't judge us.

Children's Accountability Advice to Foster Parents

- Please don't become a foster parent for the money. Check your fantasies about turning us into ideal kids.
- Remember that we want to live with families that do family things, like eating together or taking vacations. This is what a lot of us dream about.
- Please watch what you say when you are angry. Swearing may be something we have done but not something we expect from foster parents.
- Chances are that we will obey your rules when we negotiate them together.

- We may not say anything, but we watch what you say and do around other people.
- Please do not tell us what's wrong with our families. We can complain, but not you.
- Trust is a big issue and it comes over time. We do not know how long we will be with you.
- Please do not speak another language in front of us.
- Please do not go through our personal things.
- Please do not introduce us as your "adopted" or "foster" child.
- Please keep yourself informed about how you can do a better job and admit your mistakes.
- Please behave as you tell us to behave.
- Please ask us what we think before a court decision is made about our lives.
- Please do not judge us.

Building Compassion

Child welfare workers and foster parents can improve their job skills by focusing on a number of things unrelated to paperwork or other concrete examples of accountability. The motivation behind doing good work is more often internal than external.

Compassion toward others should not be confused with having loose boundaries around rules and right conduct. Arousing personal compassion awakens workers to the needs of children in a more practical way, however, it is daring, because they may experience some emotional discomfort. Here are some exercises that can help. They can be practiced alone or with friends.

Before beginning, find a quiet setting and take some deep breaths, gradually allowing your body and mind to catch up with the other. Then practice these suggestions, always remembering that you can stop at any time:

- Repeat to yourself three times, "I do not wish to be indifferent to the suffering of others."
- Repeat to yourself, "I wish to be an observer of my actions today."
- Imagine that you will be moving to another town, state, and country where you know no one.
- Think of your children or children who are close to you and imagine them going to live with strangers.
- Imagine that the children you work with do not need to suffer needlessly.
- Repeat to yourself, "I wish that the children I look after will experience my love today."
- Repeat to yourself, "I will try to know the deepest hurts of my most difficult clients."
- Imagine yourself walking into a room full of strangers and being asked personal questions about people you love such as, "Does anyone in your family drink or use drugs?" "Has anyone ever touched you in your private area?" "Has your mother ever hurt you?"
- Repeat to yourself three times, "I wish to be free of my anger."

We Can Be Better Workers by Following These Simple Principles

Job accountability goes beyond the ability to fill out paperwork and complete intervention plans. Because accountability in child welfare is about building relationships, a good worker never views children, youth, or families as subordinates. This applies to other professionals as well, because teamwork is essential in helping children. Although using accountability principles is synonymous with common sense, in a busy world, they can sometimes seem difficult to follow. Here are some other guidelines:

- Take responsibility for mistakes and don't blame others. This behavior shows willingness to learn and grow with the job.

- Give clients an opportunity whenever possible to set their own goals.

- Use constructive words and phrases when expressing disappointment in someone's behavior, such as, "This is not the behavior from someone so creative."

- Make time to be accessible to coworkers as well as clients when they are going through rough times.

- Let people know they are visible by your acknowledgments. Smile and offer a pleasant hello.

- Be on the lookout to spot good behavior that you can praise. Give immediate credit to that person in front of others. You may even want to photograph them.

- Never let sloppy work go unchecked with yourself and those you supervise.

- Share meals or coffee with your clients and coworkers.

- After completing a goal or an assignment with a client send them a note of congratulations.

- Try to get to know your supervisor and his or her work style and goals. You will be able to anticipate his or her needs and demonstrate your ability to follow direction.

- Be dependable with coworkers as well as clients. Your team members and your clients need to rely on you. Both feel unsafe around inconsistency. Although honest mistakes are likely to be tolerated, unreliable behavior can be extremely frustrating to others.

- Be diplomatic by carefully choosing your words. Think before speaking.

- Do not share personal problems with clients.

- Be aware when you speak ill of others. It is natural to assume that if someone speaks poorly about others, they may do the same thing about the listener.

- Try to create an atmosphere of free communication with your clients by losing any defensiveness. Consider their suggestions and comments, while setting rules around respectful communication.

Tips for Supporting Foster Families

Family Support America, a national nonprofit agency, offers these suggestions on how to work best with foster families ("Tips for Supporting," 2001):

- *Reduce intrusions into families' homes. Whenever possible, give families a choice about whether services are provided in the home or at another location, schedule meeting times convenient for the family, consolidate visits as much as possible, and be on time for appointments.*

- *Appreciate foster families' efforts. Spend extra time gaining trust before making suggestions about alternative parenting styles or questioning their integrity.*

- *Help families cope with transitions. Help families express their feelings when saying goodbye to a child. Be supportive when they discuss their concerns. Introduce them to other foster families going through the same experience and support all family members.*

- *Acknowledge the sacrifices made by family members. Help foster parents to recognize when their birthchildren are struggling with jealousy, frustration, and anger. Help them reassure their birthchildren. Appreciate their role in providing a safe, temporary home for another child.*

- *Listen to frustrations. Acknowledge how difficult working directly with birthfamilies can be at times and refer them to special services, such as family therapy.*

Child Welfare Accountability in the New Century Requires Self-Responsibility

Although measuring child welfare initiatives through sophisticated evaluation tools is strongly emphasized, true worker accountability begins with individual character. The effectiveness of child welfare in the 21st century as a whole depends on how we all conduct ourselves. Being willing to look inward to move beyond our fears will create success. Authentic accountability requires that we take responsibility for our mistakes as we continue to advocate in behalf of clients.

References

Canedy, D. (2002, July 1). Children suffer as Florida agency struggles. *The New York Times*, 1.

DCF to dismiss 3 counselors for falsifying records. (2002, June 13). *Florida Times Union*, B4.

Hillman, J. (1999). *The force of character.* New York: Ballantine.

Tips for supporting foster families: Family support fact sheet. (2001). Chicago: Family Support America.

Other Resources

Bhushan, P. (1999). *On leadership.* Bangalore, India: Andhra Pradesh.

Chodron, P. (2001). *The places that scare you; A guide to fearlessness in difficult times.* Boston: Shambhala Classics.

Cook, R. (2002, July 8). *Reform curbs appetite for locking kids up.* Washington, DC: Coalition for Juvenile Justice.

De Nicolas, A. T. (1986). *Powers of imagining.* Albany, NY: Ignatius de Loyola, State University of New York Press.

Dhal, P. (1999). *Human values, the heart of dynamic parenting.* Canberra, Australia: Global Service.

LaCorte, R. (2002, June). DCF worker charged with faking records. *Florida Times Union*, A1.

Pinkham, P. (2002, June 27). DCF managers at fault, poll says. *Times Union*, B1.

Policies and procedures manual. (2003, January). Washington, DC: U.S. Department of Health & Human Services,

Sharp, D. (2002, June 14). Florida cases symbolize meltdown of child welfare. *USA Today*, A1.

CHAPTER 6

Understanding Cultural Competence from a 21st-Century Perspective

Cultural Competence Isn't What It Used to Be

> I believed that since I had the knowledge I could be clinically sensitive to other cultures. I soon found that this belief was very erroneous.
> —*Lawless (2002)*

Cultural competence has become a major consideration for child welfare workers in the 21st century. Our country is awakening to its abundant diversity and its ethnic and social treasures. Child welfare addresses cultural competence in a variety of ways. Federal, state, and local child welfare grant applications pay particular attention to cultural competence. Furthermore, people representing nondominant cultures are more often able to advocate for themselves. Foster parenting and adoption by gay and lesbian couples has also been brought to the caregiver arena. Debate continues on the appropriateness of adopting children who are racially different from their prospective parents.

Discrimination Reports

Although improvements have occurred since the 1950s, serious problems still occur with regard to children and discrimination. Racial injustice is particularly seen in juvenile justice systems. Youth of color are treated more harshly than white youth for the same crimes in detention, processing in juvenile court, transfer to adult criminal court, sentencing, and incarceration in juvenile and adult facilities. Courts committed African American youth with no prior drug offenses to state institutions 48 times as often as white youth with no prior drug offenses. They sentenced African American youth 90 days longer for violent offenses than white youth. Latino youth stay 150 days longer.

Discrimination is the denial of equal treatment. In a CWLA study (2002b), 48% of children ages 8 to 11 and 67% of children 12 to 15 stated that children at their schools were treated badly because they were "different" and that discrimination was a big problem for people their age in school. In 1999, 7,876 hate crimes were reported in the United States. Nearly two-thirds of all known perpetrators were teenagers or young adults (CWLA, 2002b).

The cultural sensitivity message was brought home in the last decade. More people discovered their voices and were heard. Others rediscovered their cultural roots. In an effort to affirm races, faiths, and sexual orientations, federal and state governments worked at validating these issues on almost every level.

More than a few social service workers, however, are saying that we have missed the mark by becoming too politically sensitive. Dr. Killough, an expert in cultural ecological systems, has commented that people now have a "heightened sensitivity where we can't be sensitive." The task in applying this new sensitivity to child welfare work is in understanding cultural competence from a less generalized perspective. Perhaps this means that we need to speak more openly about our uniqueness and refrain from lumping children and families into ethnic boxes.

Dr. Killough alludes to the idea that under the current politically correct climate, people are "polite-ing" each other to death. He cautions against becoming too sensitive, because it stops us from getting to know one another. Dr. Killough shared his feelings about one of his personal cultures when he remarked:

> I relate more to my agricultural background. I don't relate to the stereotypical idea of an African American man. My cultural roots are in the South. My early rising habits, my love of nature as a way to self-renew define more about who I am. I object when someone wants to put me into an urban, black male slot or call me an "Uncle Tom."

No one enjoys being stereotyped. Workers often walk a fine line between stereotyping and demonstrating cultural competence. Yet categorizing people and cultures is a natural first step in becoming aware that not everyone thinks and behaves the same.

What Is Culture?

In this chapter, we define *culture* as a framework for making human connections. Historically, people have defined cultures by their internal and external conditions. For example, *Americanism* is a culture. As Americans, we are affected by external conditions, such as the global economy and U.S. foreign policy. An internal American condition is our individual patriotism or our political leanings.

A family is a culture that provides a framework for building connections as well. One way to define a family culture is externally, by gender, race, income, history, and so forth. A way to define a family culture internally is through its shared values and norms. These commonalties compel the family members to behave a certain way. The connections within our families influence our beliefs, behaviors, world view, and social domain.

Two families from the same neighborhood may be entirely different. Kids from one family may know their neighbors and be even looked after by community members. Children from another family, living on the same street, may be socially isolated and overly controlled by their caregivers. Both families may have working parents, shared ethnicity, and similar income. These families are culturally categorized by their external influences when workers fill out paperwork. Good workers, however, understand the tremendous effect of internal influences as well. External culture influences provide a framework, but internal ones help us understand why people are unique.

In America, culture has been viewed largely from a westernized perspective. This situation has influenced child welfare's treatment of children and families. A westernized view not based on oral traditions, but rather on written ones, emphasizes categorizing groups more than paying attention to individual group members.

This categorizing or grouping can lead, at times, to making general assumptions about complex problems. For example, people have truly believed that the phrase "just say no to drugs" could solve the addiction problem in America. This thinking was also behind expectations that if children were placed in "proper homes," they would forget about their traumatic experiences and get over their emotional outbursts.

Child welfare workers must move beyond making basic assumptions about youth by digging deeper into the causes of their problems. For instance, a first generation 10-year old Korean American child can be cared for by Korean-speaking or non-Korean-speaking parents. If workers stop their inquiry at the external framework of "Korean," they can make erroneous assumptions about this child and family. If they begin to ask about immigrant versus assimilated parenting, however, they can begin to understand what it means to be culturally aware.

An Increase in Non-English-Speaking Children

School age children who speak a language other than English at home and have trouble speaking English have nearly doubled over the last 20 years, increasing from 2.8% in 1979 to 5% in 1999 ("America's Children," 2002).

Biology Culture and Cultural Competence

Cultural competence is the ability to demonstrate thoughtful attitudes and behaviors toward others. The broad definition adopted by one national child welfare organization defines cultural competence in child welfare as

> *the ability of individuals and systems to respond respect-*
> *fully and effectively to people of all cultures, races, ethnic*
> *backgrounds, sexual orientations, and faiths or religions*

in a manner that recognizes, affirms, and values the worth of individuals, families, tribes, and communities and protects the dignity of each. (Malik & Velázquez, 2002)

The definition is global and compassionate, however, it does not address how child welfare workers can figure out a child's complete cultural orientation and, thus, his or her true needs. Cultural competence is more than just respecting a child's ethnic link. Workers can empower their clients and families when they understand how children are nurtured in their families. Uncovering past and current nurturing reveals children's individual natures. In fine-tuning work with children, workers need to recognize the effect of neurobiology on a human being's internal culture.

One evolving internal cultural theory in the 21st century relates to human biology. The Human Genome Project is exploding old assumptions about cultures and leading to a new frontier of identifying individuals by their genetics. Neurological research is expanding understanding about dominant regions of the brain that guide human behavior. Consequently, child welfare workers in the 21st century need to be familiar with human biology culture when intervening with children.

In becoming culturally competent, workers must remain open to the idea that they are working with a number of cultures when they work with children. They need to learn their clients' ethnic and family cultures as well as their individual biology cultures. They should read the UN Convention on the Rights of the Child for more information (see following page).

Two Children with Similar Ethnic Backgrounds

Janet, a child protective service worker, recently moved from Indiana to northern New Mexico. Having visited the area before her move, she was aware that many children of Native American and Spanish American descent live in the region. In her first week on the job, she received two new files. One file belonged to 6-year-old Martin, and the other pertained to David, age 14. Their files revealed some similarities.

Martin

Martin's mother was raised on an American Indian reservation in northern New Mexico. His father's family had lived in the region for centuries and had been traced to Spanish explorers. Martin's dad was arrested for mak-

---

1989 UN Convention on Rights of the Child

The UN Convention on the Rights of the Child (CRC) states that children of ethnic, religious, or linguistic minorities or of indigenous origin should not be denied the right to enjoy their culture, practice their own religion, or use their own language with other members of their group. CRC calls for children to be educated to help them develop respect for their own cultural identity, language, and values and for civilizations different from their own. Workers should prepare children to live in the spirit of understanding, peace, tolerance, equality of sexes, and friendship among all ethnic, national, and religious groups (Malik & Velázquez, 2002).

---

ing methamphetamine in a laboratory behind their house. The court sentenced him to prison and placed Martin's mother on probation. The children were assigned to protective services. Martin still lived with his mom and brothers, but he was becoming uncontrollable. Janet would be monitoring Martin and his family for a minimum of six months.

David

David's father was Native American and his mother's family emigrated from Mexico when she was 10. His parents divorced when David, an only child, was 5. He lived full-time with his mentally ill mother and saw his father once a month. When he was 10, children's services placed him with his father and paternal grandmother. His dad worked two jobs. And his grandmother, a woman who practiced a traditional American Indian lifestyle died, when David was 13. After her death, David spent most of his time alone. He became despondent and one day attempted suicide. Janet was assigned to supervise David's progress for at least six months.

After reading their files, Janet could assume that Martin and David had a lot in common because they both came from northern New Mexico and shared Native American and Hispanic parentage. Her assumptions may be false, however. One erroneous assumption could be that David's mother's mental illness had little effect on his current depression. Another false assumption might be that Martin's parents were neglectful. Demonstrating cultural competence implores Janet to consider a number of other issues when she formulates her intervention strategies.

First, Janet recognizes that in spite of other shared cultural backgrounds, Martin and David are very different. Next, she must consider how each child was nurtured from birth to understand what prompted his behavior. As she begins to understand how the child was stimulated or not stimulated to develop neuronal pathways about coping and self-perception, she can formulate her plans.

Janet may also determine her clients' needs through one of the new models that address cultural competence from a biological perspective. This model is based on examining a child's sensitized neural centers and is called *bioculture.*

Bioculture—A 21st-Century Culture Theory

Understanding Cultural Competence from a 21st-Century Perspective

Many people believe that in the 21st-century child welfare workers will consider a child's biology culture as much as they will learn about his or her race, ethnic, and gender cultures. Neuroscientists have brought us into the neurobiology loop and have compelled workers to look at culture through their lenses.

Dr. Maria Colavito (1995) has taught and written extensively about cultural competence. Through her work, she has designed a bioculture paradigm based on neuroscience. Her theory suggests that an individual's bioculture is composed of a world view, personality traits, and crisis/stress triggers that are specific to a particular intelligence center most exercised in the brain. Thus, people who share the same dominant or sensitized intelligent center share the same bioculture.

Colavito's (1995) bioculture model takes into account the sensitivities of the developing brains in children. She theorizes that a child's past and current experiences determine which center of the brain will be exercised more. Each center is responsible for a certain brain function. Depending on which center becomes dominant, world view and personality traits emerge.

For example, growth spurts occur in specific regions of the brain as children develop. If a child experiences excessive stress during a period when one of those areas is growing, he or she may later exercise that part of the brain most. If a child is traumatized before age 3, he or she could exercise the amygdala, or fear center, the part of the brain then experiencing a growth spurt. If a child experiences excessive stress while the limbic system grows, the emotion center may dominate.

Colavito (1995) identified five human biocultures. She theorized that a person's primary bioculture reflects one of these five and relates to their nurturing history. She believed that a secondary bioculture also reflects the family's projection of who they believe the person is. For instance, have you ever known a person who makes everyone laugh at work? Then, you see the person at home with siblings, and he or she seems like a different person. You have observed the person's primary and secondary biocultures.

The five biocultures include the survival bioculture, community bioculture, creative bioculture, appeal to authority bioculture, and rationale bioculture (Colavito, 1995):

Survival Bioculture—Exercises the Amygdala and Septal Region of the Limbic System ("You're with Me or Against Me")

This bioculture exercises the fear circuitry of the brain. When this area is dominant, the child's world view is skewed by fear. His or her issues are fear of abandonment, survival, and trust. A survival bioculture child will scan the environment for personal safety. He or she goes into crisis when he or she perceives or is actually abandoned. Children who have been victims of early sexual abuse or children with ADHD can be from the survival bioculture.

Community Bioculture—Exercises the Limbic System/Hippocampus and Prefrontal Cortex ("One for All and All for One")

This bioculture exercises the emotional circuitry of the brain. When this area is dominant, the world view focuses on communal welfare. Issues are community versus loneliness as well as the importance of listening to family stories. A community bioculture child lives in the moment, and what is true now may not be true for him or her in the future. These children scan their environment for changing circumstances that will dictate a change in their behavior. Their crisis is triggered when they feel they are being falsely labeled or categorized. Children from alcoholic or drug-addicted parents or poor but close immigrant families can be in the community bioculture.

Creative Bioculture—Exercises the Right Hemisphere of the Neocortex ("Always Try to Be Your Best")

This bioculture exercises the visual circuitry of the brain. When this area is dominant, the child's world view focuses on visual perception and objects. Issues are perfectionism versus fear of rejection. Reality is based on trying to keep appearances in line with an idealized internal image of the world. Creative bioculture children set and demand high standards while they create high standards. They can also be visionaries. These children scan their environment for imperfections and are constantly striving for the perfect world. Their crisis is triggered by being rejected or having their work rejected. Examples of creative bioculture youth can be those who have experienced trauma a little later in their lives and have learned to cope by using their imaginations or creative abilities.

Appeal to Authority Bioculture—Exercises the Left Hemisphere of the Neocortex ("I Obey the Rules!")

This bioculture exercises the "theory-making" brain circuitry. Children from this bioculture have issues that have to do with competence versus alienation from authority figures. They sacrifice their hearts for their heads. Appeal to authority youth search for the latest theory, belief, or authority to validate their opinions. Their crisis occurs when they experience alienation from authority figures. Children from this culture were forced to compromise their natural inclinations to accommodate a larger authority agent. Children who have been placed in military schools, are cult members, or are reformed deviants can reflect from the appeal to authority bioculture.

Rationale Bioculture—Exercises the Amygdala and Interpreter Module in the Left Hemisphere of the Neocortex ("There's No Such Thing as Bad Press")

This bioculture exercises the brain circuitry that superimposes fear over reality while using scapegoats to validate perceptions. The issues for rationale bioculture children are emotional or physical deprivation. They attempt to gain attention through arguing and projection. They use technology to act out their fantasies. Their crisis occurs when they are ignored. Rationale bioculture kids may have experienced early neglect and little or no bonding or attachment. They have not been able to use creative alternatives to compensate for their deprivation. They acquired early fear conditioning without further development of their imaginative or creative intelligence centers. Early interaction with technology, such as computers, became substitutes. Children with attachment and conduct disorders can be from the rationale bioculture. These children can become dangerous because they have difficulty feeling remorse and magically believe they can use technology to destroy things.

Colavito (1995) believes that when we recognize biocultures, we increase our cultural competence. Consequently, she feels that workers can plan interventions to match a child's bioculture. For example, if a child has a rationale bioculture, he or she will need a good deal of re-parenting matched with a healthy respect for the child's need for space. If a child represents the appeal to authority bioculture, he or she could be sensitive to rejection. Workers need to be aware not to disrupt the child's routines by appearing at school without first letting him or her know.

Back to Martin and David

When Janet began to investigate Martin's and David's histories, she learned a lot. She discovered that Martin was nurtured by both parents and that he was traumatized when his father went to prison. He scribbled on walls and destroyed his toys. Janet soon recognized that he was a creative bioculture child, so she referred him and his mother to a family therapist who knew how to teach children about using their creativity to cope with loss. Janet's professional mask with Martin was to be playful.

When Janet dug deeper into David's history, she found that his birth-mother had sexually molested him when he was 5 and that his paternal grandmother's use of traditional Indian rituals helped him feel safe. Janet concluded that David was from the survival bioculture. She helped David's father understand that safety is a central issue with trauma survivors and that David should be seeing a trauma specialist. Her professional mask with David was to be soft-spoken and careful about introducing abrupt changes in his life.

Bioculture Theory Can Apply to Families

Because families are composed of members with individual nurturing histories, each family may acquire its own bioculture. Yet what happens when a mother with an appeal to authority bioculture has a teenager with a creative bioculture? If the mother discovers her 16-year-old daughter's erotic poetry, she may confront her child. Her daughter may become angry, not only because her mother found her writing, but also because her mother judged its content.

Workers should emphasize the strengths inherent in each bioculture and use them to help family members make connections. One of the strengths in the appeal to authority bioculture is the adherence to following rules. A strength in the previous example is the mother's dedication to conventional thinking about mothering. Her daughter's strength could be her writing. The mother and daughter may connect with one other when they both recognize that the mother needs to be appreciated for trying to be a good mom and her daughter needs recognition for her writing talent.

Being Culturally Aware Through Recognition and Practice

Colavito's (1995) theory complements new discoveries in neuroscience and could help child welfare workers better understand children and families. It is also helpful to understand current cultural competence material. The National Center for Cultural Competence, Georgetown University (2002), created a checklist intended to heighten cultural awareness, a sample of which follows:

> You can respond to any of the comments by answering (a) things I do frequently, (b) things I do occasionally, or (c) things I do rarely or never. The checklist has no answer key with correct responses. If the respondent frequently marked C, however, he or she might not demonstrate culturally competent practices.

> • I display pictures, posters, or other materials that reflect the cultures and ethnic backgrounds of children and families served by my program or agency.

- *When using videos, films, or other media resources for health education, treatment, or other interventions, I ensure that they reflect the cultures of children and families served by my program or agency.*

- *I ensure that toys and other play accessories...are representative of the various cultural and ethnic groups within the local community and the society in general.*

- *For children who speak languages or dialects other than English, I attempt to learn and use key words in their language so I am better able to communicate with them during assessment, treatment, or other interventions.*

- *I recognize and accept that individuals from culturally diverse backgrounds may desire varying degrees of acculturation into the dominant culture.*

- *I accept and respect that male-female roles in families may vary significantly among different cultures.*

- *I accept that religion and other beliefs may influence how families respond to illnesses, disease, disability, and death.*

- *Before visiting or providing services in the home setting, I seek information on acceptable behaviors, courtesies, customs, and expectations that are unique to families of specific cultures and ethnic groups served by my program or agency.*

- *I advocate for the review of my program's agency's mission statement, goals, policies, and procedures to ensure that they incorporate principles and practices that promote cultural diversity and cultural competence.*

Many excellent books have enlightened child welfare workers about different cultures. Although it is extremely useful to understand them, workers must learn the biological histories of each child as well. Becoming culturally competent requires us to wear many masks. In the 21st century, biology culture is the newest one, helping complete the cultural competence picture.

Ten Things You Can Do to Promote Cultural Competence

1. Learn about the dimensions of culture in child welfare.

2. Learn about the cultural groups in communities served by your agency.

3. Include culture and cultural competence principles in the strategic planning, policy development, program design, and service delivery process.

4. Promote cultural competence through staff development, training, hiring, retention, career advancement, performance evaluations, and policies.

5. Create a safe environment in which staff feel comfortable discussing cultural competence.

6. Become involved in community boards and cultural activities.

7. Hire people who reflect diversity in your community.

8. Advocate for cultural competence in other groups that affiliate with your agency.

9. Mediate cultural competence discussions.

10. Make your agency's recreational activities reflective of all cultural groups.

Source: Child Welfare League of America (2002a).

References

America's children, 2001. (2002, May 19). Available from http://www.Childstats.gov/ac2001/ac01.asp.

Child Welfare League of America. (2002a, February 12). *Cultural competence.* Washington, DC: Author.

Child Welfare League of America. (2002b). *Making children a national priority: A framework for community action.* Washington, DC: Author.

Colavito, M. M. (1995). *The heresy of Oedipus and the mind/mind split: A study of the biocultural origins of civilization.* Lewiston, NY: Edwin Mellin Press.

Lawless, J. (2002, March/April). A Caucasian male's journey. *Family Therapy Magazine, 1*(2), 24–29.

Malik, S., & Velázquez, J., Jr. (2002). Cultural competence and the "new Americans." *Children's Voice, 11*(4), 24–26.

National Center for Cultural Competence, Georgetown University Center for Child and Human Development, Georgetown University. (1999–2002). *Self-assessment checklist for personnel providing services and support to children with special health needs and their families.* Washington, DC: Author.

Additional Resources

Compo-Flores, A. (2002, July 1). Macho or sweetness. *Newsweek,* 51.

de Nicolas, A. (1989). *Habits of mind.* New York: Authors' Choice Press.

Gender perspectives. (2002, July/August). *Family Therapy Magazine, 1*(4).

Locke, D. C. (1998). *Increasing multicultural understanding: A comprehensive model.* Thousand Oaks, CA Sage.

Paniagua, F. A. (1998). *Assessing and treating culturally diverse clients: A practical guide.* Thousand Oaks, CA: Sage.

Teicher, M. H. (2002, July 1). Scars that won't heal: The neurobiology of child abuse. *Scientific American, 2*(4), 68–75.

Weaver, H. N. (1998, May). *Indigenous people in a multicultural society: Unique issues for human services.* Washington, DC: National Association of Social Workers.

CHAPTER 7

Preventing Workplace Problems

What Do Employers Want? I Think I Know, But I'm Not Sure

> When we begin to take our failures non-seriously, it means we are ceasing to be afraid of them. It is of immense importance to learn to laugh at ourselves.

—*Katherine Mansfield, Writer*

We spend approximately 2,000 hours at our jobs every year. Our work environment frequently becomes a home away from home where friendships are cemented and meaningful activities take place. Although we cannot control a lot about our work tasks, we can learn to avoid unnecessary problems if we are aware of common workplace mistakes. Understanding how to accent our skills and staying away from avoidable trouble at work is key to a successful career in child welfare.

"Political correctness" on the job was a guiding phrase in the 1990s. It may seem self-explanatory, but it can be confusing. This is because political correctness is different depending on where we live and work. Although it may be fine to address a coworker one way in Texas, the appropriate term may be quite different in New York City. Consequently, workers are challenged to understand a number of things about the work site's culture when they begin a new job.

This chapter will discuss why child welfare workers sometimes get into trouble at work. It begins with a review of federal, state and local laws that were created for workers' benefit.

Workplace Equal Rights

Laws have been instituted to protect workers. They include the Fair Labor & Standards Act, the Americans with Disabilities Act, the Civil Rights Act, and the Age Discrimination Act. Human resource departments within agencies keep copies of them.

In addition, every work site should post a code of ethics and mission statement. Employment manuals should include agency policies and guidelines, as well as corrective action procedures. Policies include dress and language guidelines, whereas corrective action procedures discuss disciplinary protocol. Review them all before deciding if a job is right for you, because they reflect an agency's priorities.

If supervisors are doing their job, they can tell how a new worker is acclimating within three months. Hiring systems are designed to evaluate employees for the first 30, 60, and 90 days. Child welfare agencies generally have a probationary period so that both worker and employer can recognize if the job is a good fit. Employers are at a disadvantage if they are unable to spot potential problems before the probationary period is over because it is more difficult to let a worker go after a long period than after a few months.

Have Child Welfare Workers Changed?

Many child welfare administrators and supervisors feel that the workplace has changed over the years. Here is a sampling of their observations:

- **Constant shifts in the workplace have created greater professional mobility and placed more responsibility for career advancement on the individual versus the employer.** Changing funding streams and strained caseloads can compel workers to look for more rewarding work or opportunities for advancement in other agencies. In years past, many child welfare workers progressed through the same agency. Today, agencies often hire new administrators from outside, or administrators move horizontally through the interagency system. In addition, some administrators report that workers seem to be more·restless, expect quick advancement, demand more income, and want new challenges before they have acquired the experience or skills.

What Do Employers Want?

According to the National Association of Colleges and Employers, the five top qualities employers want are:

- good oral and written communication skills,

- honesty and integrity,

- teamwork,

- interpersonal skills, and

- strong work ethic.

Other employers cite the abilities to learn, demonstrate initiative, and make decisions. Most employers know that many students do not leave college with the ability to do the job initially, so having a desire to learn and grow from mistakes is another essential quality (Collins, 2001).

- **Workers are less willing to make concessions that would intrude on personal time.** Across the board, all professions have become clearer about workers' personal time. It has become a priority.

- **Support systems for workers have eroded because there is less money and time to access them.** Many supervisors and administrators are frustrated by the scarcity of time that inhibits workers from making connections within their agency. In the past, mentors guided new workers and helped continue their education. Now, in many places, continuing education has been curtailed or is no longer underwritten. Agencies provide fewer education incentives, and people take less time to mentor.

- **Some workers challenge administrators because they may feel entitled to pay raises without merit and express resentment when supervisors correct their mistakes.** One administrator remarked that unlike some child welfare workers now, he would never have asked for excessive amounts of time off or spoken disrespectfully to supervisors when he began working 25 years ago. He also commented that he did not understand why some new workers believe they know more than their boss. One human resource director said, "A single internship does not compare to 15 years of experience." His remarks reflect the views of many senior staff members. Another agency CEO commented about a new worker who complained to him that her supervisor, with 30 years of experience and authorship of several books, did not treat her as a peer. The administrator informed his new employee that she was not her supervisor's professional peer.

- **Workers are more diverse.** Child welfare workers represent a greater range of cultures, religions, and sexual orientations, or at least have opportunities to disclose them with less fear of retribution. More workers are freer to discuss ethnic or religious diversity as they feel more comfortable expressing their needs.

- **Male workers are demonstrating more careful behavior through their discussions and actions.** Sexual harassment lawsuits have created a larger sensitivity by men about inappropriate workplace behavior. Supervisors and administrators, however, remarked that women are becoming bolder with their comments about personal issues. Consequently, women may feel somewhat empowered, whereas men feel confused. For example, one child welfare worker talked about his awkwardness as women in the lunchroom described their monthly menstrual cycles.

- **Worker tasks have equalized.** Thirty years ago, it was not unusual to require women, but not men, to take typing tests during a job interview. Now, men and women generally share tasks within the office.

- **Male and female workers share equal pay.** Pay was slanted more in men's directions in the past, and even if an agency set a pay scale, administrators often developed "extenuating circumstances" to justify men's higher salaries. This justification was intended to keep men working in child welfare, because there has always been a dearth of male workers. Women still represent most of the child welfare workforce, but strict federal guidelines help ensure equal pay for everyone.

- **Workers are more vulnerable to false accusations by angry parents or guardians.** The increasingly litigious U.S. society contributes to the fact that workers are vulnerable to accusations of abuse within treatment settings. Even when allegations are blazingly false, workers can be stigmatized for the remainder of their careers.

This Story Happens Often

Jake had spent 20 years in the military before leaving to work in the civilian community. He had experienced success in his previous work but felt that he wanted to contribute more to society after his retirement. He interviewed for a job with a local child welfare agency working with adolescent youth in a residential treatment facility.

When he began working, he was dismayed by his coworkers' seemingly lackadaisical attitudes toward their own dress and language. At staff meetings, he was further upset, because he felt that some of the younger staff were disrespectful toward the center's administrator.

Over time, he voiced some of these opinions, and his comments were met with resentment by a few of the other workers. They felt Jake was uptight and judgmental, although he seemed to have a good rapport with the kids.

While on duty one day, a 14-year-old resident exploded after Jake asked him to take a time-out in his room. The youth barreled toward Jake, knocking him against a wall. Jake ducked just as the boy's fist hit the stucco wall, causing severe bruising and requiring a trip to the hospital to x-ray his hand.

After hearing what happened, the young man's mother and stepfather accused Jake of abusing their son. The agency was required to follow up on a child abuse complaint through their human resources department as well as cooperate with a child abuse investigation.

Coworkers disgruntled by Jake in the past began to build on sketchy information, and soon rumors expanded around the allegations. Jake had counted on his administrator to support him unconditionally, and rather than openly vocalizing her support, she seemed concerned about a lawsuit.

Office Problems

The following are ways supervisors can handle office problems.

• Do not ignore conflicts, because they are red flags that reflect staff morale and team-building problems.

• Encourage workers to take responsibility for working out their own conflicts, but follow up by asking them how they reconciled the situation. Redirect people to speak directly with one another so that splitting between staff members is avoided.

• Look for the core issues behind conflicts, and be careful not to assume that it is a personality issue. Workers can become extremely frustrated if they feel their supervisors are being superficial.

• Solve conflicts with the parties alone, not in front of other workers. Never force a group to confront a worker.

• Be a coach before stepping into a conflict.

• Telling a group to stop complaining will not resolve an issue. Confront a chronic complainer alone. Chronic complainers are difficult because they do a lot of damage. Other workers expect supervisors to take a stand with this type of individual. If a complainer affects morale and disrupts the work environment, you have a responsibility to discuss his or her disruptive behavior.

The investigation took weeks to resolve because the investigator needed to conduct interviews and write reports. All the while, Jake was assigned a "no contact with children" job at the agency. He began to avoid the staff lounge and spoke less at staff meetings. He felt that even his closest supporters were wary of him. He was humiliated and frustrated.

Finally, the investigator recorded the physical abuse allegation as unfounded. Yet, Jake thought it was a hollow victory. He had been hurt by rumors, felt abandoned by his boss, and wondered how he would regain the trust of coworkers. Within a month, he left the job.

Jake's story, although a compilation of worker experiences, is a child welfare worker's nightmare. Workers are increasingly vulnerable these days to false reports made by disgruntled guardians or youth, and although investigation methods have also improved, the stigma associated with any false allegation is difficult to live down.

- **Workers are using flex hours and job sharing to continue working after the birth of children or to accommodate complicated job tasks.** With the increased use of computers, many workers are able to complete paperwork from their homes. Job sharing is another way to keep continuity with clients as teams of workers can help one another to complete work assignments. Employers are beginning to understand that being creative and flexible can keep valued professionals on the job.

- **Both child welfare workers and administrators are more fearful of taking decisive actions due to political ramifications.** Workers, as well as their supervisors, have been more careful about making decisive comments or taking action. Child welfare agencies must not only please politicians, they must bow to the whims of board members. Often, agency boards are composed of influential people in the community with good intentions but limited knowledge about what is best for children. For example, instead of saying, "The child's parents aren't responsible," workers or administrators may now say, "We must consider the birthparents as well as the safety of their children." Or in lieu of remarking, "Why don't our commissioners take a stand and impose a surcharge to increase worker salaries?" an administrator may say, "Understanding that a tax is difficult to impose, perhaps we need another study that assesses worker needs." And finally, "We need to do everything we can to advocate for this child's adoption" can be watered down to, "We need to consider the birthparents as much as the child when it comes to the adoption."

- **More workers have college degrees, but they have serious gaps when it comes to practical skills.** Although more child welfare workers hold undergraduate degrees, many of these degrees are not relevant to child welfare work. It is difficult for public child welfare agencies to pay social workers what they would receive in the private sector. Therefore, they hire workers with English, anthropology, history, and other degrees. Even when workers have relevant degrees, they may not have been trained in appropriate record keeping, group work, medication, trauma, or de-escalating protocols.

How to Avoid Problems at Work

Crossing Boundaries with the Wrong Person

Common sense usually leads workplace behavior. According to Greg Britton, Human Resource Director for a large human service agency, "People get into trouble by crossing boundaries with the wrong person." He thinks that when workers forget to "shift gears" they open themselves up to problems. Here are a few scenarios:

> Mary recently moved from Mississippi to Washington, D.C., to take a job as an adoptions worker. On her first day, she engaged in playful conversation with one of her Hispanic coworkers. Together, they laugh at a joke, and then Mary proceeds to share another story about a Mexican family from Mississippi. Mary had many Hispanic friends in her former state, but her colleague, unaware of this, makes some negative assumptions and expresses dissatisfaction to their supervisor.

> Gary is 50 years old. He loves to hunt, fish, and watch football games. His friends understand his somewhat antiquated comments about women. In fact, Jake has many female friends who simply roll their eyes at his sense of humor, but also know he has a big heart. A 26-year-old worker arrives on the job, and in the next few weeks is dismayed to hear that although she has never heard it directly from him, Jake has referred to her as a Barbie doll. She feels diminished by his remarks and avoids communication with him about a case they both share.

At the annual Christmas party, Nancy corners the boss's wife and tells her that she has a bone to pick with the woman's husband. They had met on one other occasion, and Nancy felt comfortable talking with her. Nancy takes the wife's silence as a sign to continue voicing her views and names other staff members at the same agency who are upset with her husband as well. The following week, Nancy is called into her boss's office and asked to share her complaints with him only. Her colleagues are upset when they are asked to meet with him too.

Avoid Spiritual and Political Misfires

Knowing how to adjust one's communication around people with different religions or political attitudes is a good way to stay out of trouble at work. One agency director told this story:

One of our counselors felt compelled to spread his faith among the staff. Other workers were mildly irritated at first, but became upset over time as the counselor began to engage clients in his prayer groups during work hours. This was way off the mark when it came to appropriate professional behavior, and we had to take corrective action. To this day, the man feels persecuted.

Another worker spoke of her colleague, who thought it was funny to plaster his favorite candidate's bumper stickers on coworkers' desks. It can be troublesome to bring politics to the office. Leave it outside because it can distance workers and supervisors.

Just Say No to Workplace Romance

Because child welfare work can be intense, people often build strong bonds with coworkers. Romances have bloomed and died on the child welfare vine for more than a few people. They can destroy careers, interfere with established personal relationships, lower morale, and split other staff members:

Mary was director of a county child welfare program and had lived with her partner for more than 20 years. The agency grew under Mary's direction, and staff liked her down-to-earth style of managing. A new, married worker named Ruth arrived on the job and found that she and Mary shared a lot in common. Within six months, Ruth and Mary became close friends, and to the exclusion of other staff, traveled to conferences together and met for dinner or lunch. After a while, Ruth confided to a few coworkers that she and Mary had a romantic fling. Eventually, more people learned about their affair. Subsequently, Ruth and her husband divorced, and the agency's board members fired Mary, who continued to live with her roommate in relative seclusion.

Allison was attracted to her colleague, Alfred. They were both new to child welfare work and shared similar experiences on the job. They began to meet for coffee or breakfast. On Saturdays, Alfred sometimes stopped by Allison's house to drop off doughnuts or help her with her yardwork. Soon, they began a romantic relationship lasting six months, until Allison was promoted to a supervisory position. Alfred felt that she was taking time from him because of her new responsibilities and resented her absence. They began to argue and soon broke up. Alfred and Allison were angry at staff meetings and talked about each other's personal habits to other workers. The friendship ended.

Emotional liaisons disrupt workers' ability to support children and families and interfere with career goals. It is rare that they end happily ever after.

Avoid Ego Wars

Pride is a human condition best set aside when doing child welfare work, but unfortunately, it thrives anywhere. New workers' egos grow initially but eventually deflate as they mature into the work. Sometimes, however, they can speak irreverently about a coworker or clash with another over an opinion. Egos can get hurt when workers are ignored by a supervisor or requested to solve a problem they consider beneath their abilities.

Ego is an ugly sidekick creating a dictator within us. A retired administrator remarked that one of the toughest parts to his job was trying to finesse arrogant politicians to include a minor attachment to a child welfare bill. He knew that their decisions were seldom based on the issues themselves. Although massaging egos is often what workers do when they appeal to other professionals for help, they need to keep in mind how their own egos get involved as well.

It can also be enlightening to self-observe how personal egos are engaged when we are corrected or overruled at work. How do we handle imagined or real slights, and what do we tell ourselves about who we are when we are offended by a coworker's behavior toward us? Supervisors say that listening to constructive criticism is an asset and laughing at one's frailties is a sign of a healthy professional—a sure sign that we've been able to massage our own egos into submission.

Avoid Touching Coworkers Without Their Permission

Heightened sensitivity regarding physical touch has been brought to the workplace because people are simply becoming more self-aware. Crossing personal boundaries can sometimes be confused with sexual harassment. Because some child welfare workers are trauma survivors, they may confuse safe and unsafe touch. A friendly pat on the shoulder or head can be misconstrued if

- coworkers don't know each other very well,
- a worker is touching a formerly traumatized coworker, or
- a supervisor is trying to placate a subordinate.

It is best to wait a little while before offering hugs along with words of congratulations or consolation. Ask first when considering physically expressing yourself with a coworker.

Avoid Telling "Those Jokes" Through E-mail or in Person

The Internet has broadened our reading alternatives considerably, especially with e-mail jokes. But online joke-telling can get people into a world of trouble. For example, the Chevron Corporation paid $2.2 million dollars in damages to four female employees who were offended by the series of jokes traded via e-mail among a group of male coworkers (Taylor, 2002).

Workers are even offering jokes that people swear were not meant to offend as evidence in sexual harassment, hostile work environment, and discrimination cases. Jokes that get laughs can still sound irresponsible to juries. Some employers are even adopting humor policies.

Although laughter is universal, humor is not. People can nurse a grudge when they are offended by someone else's assumption that they share a similar sense of humor. Unfortunately, the heightened sensitivity is causing many people to tip-toe around the coffee maker.

Another e-mailing faux pas is venting about clients online. Technicians can recover these e-mails even if they are deleted, and lawyers can use them as evidence in court.

Something worse than bad humor is no humor at all, because child welfare agencies can become weak when no laughter is shared among coworkers.

Avoid Gossip

Gossip has no place in a child welfare agency, but that does not stop some people from thriving on it. People tend to gossip because they want to make a human connection, but it can diminish the speaker's credibility and damage reputations. It contributes to an unpleasant work environment for everyone. It often causes unnecessary suffering for others:

> Ted had worked for a children's agency more than 10 years. He was a hard worker and liked to converse with other employees. He spoke mostly to women at his job because there were few men, but an observing woman named Grace voiced her thoughts aloud one day when she mentioned to a colleague that Ted seemed more than platonically interested in a coworker. Her colleague began to talk to other workers, and they all concluded that Ted was romantically attracted to their friend. They eventually shared these thoughts with the woman and encouraged her to seek the advice of a lawyer. Ted's human service director learned shortly thereafter that her attorney was going to file a lawsuit against the agency for sexual harassment.

Could this lawsuit been avoided? Probably, but fueled by gossip, Ted was tried by his peers before he had an opportunity to explain or apologize for the misunderstanding. And that's if there actually was a misunderstanding. Most of the time, hearsay is not considered the truth. To succeed on the job, remain silent even when it is tempting to express your opinion.

When Do Employers Need to Take Corrective Action?

Generally, child welfare professionals can be corrected for the following reasons:

- swearing at or threatening coworkers;

- verbal or physical abuse toward clients;

- physical impropriety;

- crossing boundaries, such as sharing phone numbers with clients, asking for personal favors, exchanging money or giving loans, and having personal relationships with coworkers;

- workplace harassment;

- not completing work in a timely manner;

- disregarding other agency rules and regulations;

- intentionally interfering with the health and well-being of children;

- making serious mistakes; and

- insubordination.

Do Not Postpone Work Because "I'm Not in the Right Frame of Mind"

Allowing personal agendas and resentments to affect work performance is completely unprofessional, but some coworkers bring their moods to the office with the expectation that everyone should understand. These people can put children at risk when they delay doing their work because they are "not in the mood." Often people will tip-toe around these bullies until their attitude is corrected by supervisors. Unfortunately, supervisors, in need of workers on the job, can have a difficult time taking corrective action. Workers who allow their work performance to be affected because they are holding resentments need to rethink their commitment to helping children. Peer supervision can help to address these issues.

Avoid Harboring Jealousy

Jealousy is another human frailty. It can become a co-conspirator with one's ego. Most people can remember a time when they felt jealous of a coworker. It is hoped that the majority of us did not follow up on those feelings by doing something to thwart that person's work performance.

A typical example of using jealousy to fuel bad behavior is to take credit for another person's work. A child may have improved in her new foster placement, and at her staffing discussion, a workers could take credit for her improvement without mentioning the work accomplished by her foster parent. Another demonstration of jealousy is sniping about a coworker behind his or her back or minimize the person's achievement by rationalizing his or her rise in status. Professional jealousy plays out in a number of ways, but it can ultimately reflect poorly on our character and inhibits us from taking stock of our own weaknesses.

Take Responsibility for Your Mistakes

Making mistakes is part of the human experience. How we handle ourselves when we make mistakes, as well as the manner in which we take responsibility for them, is important. Workers in Florida who falsified their reports brought more problems on themselves by disregarding their code of conduct. They created multiple problems by not admitting their wrongful behavior when they were first questioned.

Reconciling mistakes is part of growing professionally. As a worker grows in compassion, she is less likely to feel shame and thus, deny wrongdoing. Being responsible means that we can laugh at missteps and express sincere apologies; however, one loses credibility when one avoids taking responsibility at all.

Stay Aware

Like any journey, child welfare work has its share of surprising turns, sudden obstacles, and fire-breathing dragons. A smart person is able to stay aware while carefully navigating the terrain and reading the caution signs along the way. In the long run, demonstrating restraint, discrimination, and patience leads to desired goals, and that is the best outcome when we are working in child welfare.

References

Collins, M. (2001). *What do employers want? Family support fact sheet*. Chicago: Family Support America.

Taylor, S. T. (2002, July 14). Political correctness and lawsuits make telling those jokes serious business, *Florida Times Union*, H1.

Additional Resources

Ackerman, R. H., & Maslin-Ostrouski, P. (2002). *The wounded leader*. San Francisco: Jossey-Bass.

Lloyd, J. (2002, October 7). Managers shouldn't ignore office problems. *Times Union*, 4.

Windower, R. W. (2002). *Smart hiring: The complete guide to finding and hiring the best employees* (3rd ed.). Naperville, IL: Sourcebooks.

CHAPTER 8

Understanding and Preventing Worker Burnout

Do I Have Burnout or Am I Just Fatigued by My Compassion?

A Metaphorical Story

Once upon a time, there was a beautiful princess named Doris, who lived with her parents in an enchanted castle. Every day, the princess would ride through her kingdom and enjoy the lovely hills, clear rivers, and tall trees with her faithful dog, Trooper.

One day while Doris and Trooper were out exploring, a young child appeared unexpectedly on their path. The princess and dog stopped quickly to avoid running over the boy. Doris was surprised to see that the youngster wore nothing on his feet. Doris had never seen bare feet before, and she was filled with compassion.

She asked the little boy his name. "Mark," said the child. "Well, Mark," replied Doris, "How would you like a new pair of shoes?" The little boy dimpled and assured her that he would like that very much. But added that he had brothers and sisters who needed shoes too. Doris felt sure that she could find a way to buy several pairs.

That evening, she asked her parents to loan her some money to buy the shoes. Doris's mother and father answered thoughtfully, "We don't have much money for shoes because we've built new bridges and trained more knights. We can afford to give this money only once." The naïve adults did not know that children soon grow out of shoes.

When Doris presented Mark and his family with new shoes they were delighted, but forgot to thank her. Her feelings were a little hurt. Yet, she felt warm inside. Her good deed spread throughout the kingdom, and soon she was overwhelmed with requests.

Doris worked hard to get the children what they needed. She begged for money, sponsored bake sales, and sold her tiara. She spent less time with Trooper and even forgot to celebrate her own birthday. After a while, she neglected her appearance and rarely looked in the mirror. She became irritated with anyone who suggested she take a vacation. "No!" she'd shout. "I am the only person who knows what they need."

As Doris became more exhausted, she forgot to smile or laugh. The children were frightened by her crankiness and left notes instead of stopping by to say hello. Her family and friends no longer asked her to parties or lunch. Sometimes, she cried for no reason and thought she had gone down the wrong path. She began to tell herself that she was lousy at helping kids.

One day, the exhausted princess fell asleep while she was collecting wool to make coats. She dreamed she was seated in an enchanted meadow with Trooper. To her amazement, he began to speak. "Doris, you have grown tired from your responsibilities. It is not possible to work this hard forever. To help others, you must first help yourself."

When the princess awakened, she remembered her faithful companion's message. She immediately walked home and placed a sign on the palace gates, that read, "On Break—Will Return in One Week." Then she took a long, hot bath. During her time off, she came up with some pretty good ideas about how to get help for her projects and thought about scheduling a longer vacation.

Soon, Doris and Trooper were back venturing around the kingdom. She continued to help children and grew to be a wise woman. Doris knew that caring for others and herself makes life much happier. She never forgot the words in her dream: "To help others, you must first help yourself."

Defining Child Welfare Worker Burnout

Job burnout was first identified in the 1970s and was defined as "a breakdown of psychological defenses that workers use to adapt and cope with intense job-related stressors," and "a syndrome in which a worker feels emotionally exhausted or fatigued, withdrawn emotionally from clients and perceives a diminution of achievements or accomplishments" (Kreisher, 2002). In other words, when workers experience burnout, their coping skills have declined, they are emotionally and physically drained, and they feel that what they do does not matter.

The child welfare system includes several uncontrollable factors that play a large role in feeling out of control, and loss of control is the overwhelming contributor to worker exhaustion.

Workers usually arrive at their jobs with a certain level of educational competence, an associate's, bachelor's, or master's degree. Formal training, however, does not prepare them for the challenges they can encounter. It can be jarring. The mother who beats Satan out of her children or the newborn found faintly breathing in a garbage can behind a fast food restaurant. The kids playing with parents' heroin needles, and the enraged teenager kicking in doors. The children in foster homes or hospitals claiming that nobody hurt them, it was just an accident. Policies that require workers to fight for the kids but keep themselves at emotional arm's length.

Child welfare work can mean long rides in subways and hours spent suffocating in filthy, overheated rooms. It means tolerating explosive parents and sometimes explosive judges. It can require calming a child after a 2:00 A.M. nightmare or noticing the fresh, self-inflicted wounds on another. Child advocacy can be dangerous, especially when children are removed from their homes in front of drug- or alcohol-affected parents.

While working with uncertainties, workers must also keep their feelings in check when they grieve for young clients. It is difficult to express grief if workers have no time for it and have to move on to the next case. The child welfare system is filled with workers who have not had an opportunity to deal with their losses. In an article published in *City Limits, A New York News Magazine*, a child investigations worker commented:

> The more I ended up at ECS [emergency children's services] the harder it became to comfort these children. When you had no idea where a child was going to end up that night, it was impossible to assure them of anything. When a child asks, "Am I going to get split up from my little brother?" you can't say no. Instead you have to say, "Let's hope not, okay?"

Child welfare's greatest loss is the talented people who leave the field because they are burned out. Workers' coming and going create a revolving door, especially in residential treatment. Administrators and supervisors bemoan the fact that just when a new worker is trained and beginning to give quality service, he or she leaves. The pressure is mounting as demands on people in direct service grow to reduce risk in children, fill out piles of paperwork, and live with marginal wages.

Are Burnout and Compassion Fatigue the Same?

A newer definition of worker fatigue was introduced in the last century by social researchers who studied workers who helped trauma survivors. It was called *compassion fatigue*. People confuse it with burnout, but burnout is different. Compassion fatigue or secondary traumatic stress (STS) can surface quite rapidly. Burnout, on the other hand, emerges gradually as one is exposed to mounting job strain (Figley, 1995). Burnout occurs when gradual exposure to job strain leads to an erosion of idealism, which leads to discouragement and a reduced sense of accomplishment. In Doris's story, she experienced burnout. Burnout and compassion fatigue can share symptoms, emotional exhaustion being one of them.

Unlike burnout, STS can suddenly cause a child welfare worker to feel confused, helpless, and isolated from supporters. STS symptoms are often not related to real causes. For example, one symptom is feeling worthless, reflecting irrational thinking, yet helpers with STS can experience a speedier recovery.

People with STS experience stress as a result of helping or wanting to help a suffering person in crisis. Child welfare investigation professionals may acquire STS more easily due to their early role in the child separation process. CPS professionals would be more likely to experience burnout because they tend to stay with a child's case much longer. The following page discusses a study on STS in the real world of CPS.

External and Personal Stressors

External stressors that contribute to burnout are:

- Poor agency management—Poor interoffice communication, bad managers, and constant crises in agencies contribute to low morale.

An STS Study

The *Best Practice Journal*, a publication of the National Child Welfare Resource Center for Family-Centered Practice, discussed a 1999 study assessing the prevalence and severity of STS symptoms among a sample of CPS workers in the South. It reported that up to 37% of the respondents were found to be experiencing clinical levels of emotional stress associated with STS.

- Difficult work schedules, excessive on-call hours, intense work days, and blurred job descriptions leading to a feeling of losing control, being overwhelmed, confusion, and frustration.

- Boring work, fewer opportunities for promotion, and fear of downsizing—These factors contribute to feeling stuck and not being able to realize one's potential.

- Difficult interagency politics and inadequate training—Poor or no communication between agencies or workers can lead people to make mistakes.

- Personal risk—Insufficient supervision with regard to potentially hazardous conditions places workers at risk of contracting diseases or being exposed to violent situations.

- Lack of appreciation—Everyone needs to feel good about what they do. People do not get this feeling through osmosis. Child welfare workers will leave a job sooner if they do not receive appreciation than if they receive low pay.

Personal stressors (internal) that contribute to burnout include:

- A recent loss—A loss through death, divorce, or life stage, such as children leaving home, contributes to a sense of losing control.

- Chronic illness—Ongoing sickness is exhausting and causes irritability and frustration.

- A history of trauma—Formerly traumatized workers may give their previous suffering meaning by working with children, but they may be biologically more sensitive to danger cues at work and thus experience exhaustion as a result of these physically hypervigilant conditions.

- Lack of support—Single parenting, moving to a new town, or being estranged from family can create a feeling of isolation when trying to manage home and work.

- Poor coping skills—Many people are workaholics or perfectionists. They do not know how to relax or take time to regenerate. Their communication skills may be primitive, or they may not have control over their anger.

- High expectations of others—Some workers expect their coworkers to have the same commitment to the job. If their expectations are disappointed, they become angry or withdrawn. If clients do not fulfill their treatment goals, they may become disheartened or hardened.

- Unrealistic expectations of agency administrators—A small number of child welfare workers may rebel against authority and pout when they do not get their way. Their obsession with trying to change the system can exhaust them.

- Choosing the wrong career—Child welfare work is not for everyone. People who want to please others can choose it for the wrong reasons. Dealing with the resulting conflicting feelings puts tremendous strain on physical and emotional systems.

Burnout Symptom Categories

According to Figley (1995), burnout has five symptom categories: physical, emotional, behavioral, work-related, and interpersonal.

Physical and Emotional Symptoms

Chronic stress can create linked physical and emotional symptoms in child welfare workers. Chapter 2 discussed the effects of stress on the brain, creating neural changes that can desensitize the body. Scholar Antonio deNicolas believes that burnout occurs when workers no longer feel sensations. They become numb to their surroundings and depersonalize experiences. For instance, they forget to be careful and may end up calling their supervisor a name or telling a traumatized child to "snap out of it," or they lose their compassion.

At the same time, workers' bodies can become hypersensitive to cues that trigger fight or flight responses. Although they are physically hyperalert or numb, they can also be overly expressive or emotionally distant.

Formerly traumatized child welfare workers can make excellent professionals, but they may be at risk of becoming burned out because their bodies have developed sensitivity to danger triggers. Before they became child welfare workers, their physical systems were conditioned to be more alert.

Over time, any child welfare worker can acquire other physical or emotional symptoms that include:

- sleep disturbances;

- irritability;

- detached interest in activities;

- weak immune system;

- headaches, indigestion, colds, and flu;

- difficulty concentrating;

- depression;

- feelings of helplessness;

- anxiety;

- guilt;

- exhaustion; and

- substance abuse.

Behavioral Symptoms

Aggression, voiced cynicism, substance abuse, and defensiveness are behavioral characteristics associated with burnout. Chronic stress can create a gradual change in behavior. People seldom recognize their own decline until they catch ourselves getting unreasonably angry or crying uncontrollably. For one worker, it was a life-changing experience.

Clara's Story

I've worked with kids all my life. When I began in child welfare, I was on a mission to save the world. Some social work schools require their students get therapy. Mine didn't. Big mistake, because I was totally unaware about how much my childhood affected me.

When I entered the field, I soon learned that my high expectations for changing the world needed to be lowered, but I was stubborn. I kept thinking that if I only pushed one way or the other, all the children on my caseload would either get the help they needed or realize that I was their best friend. I was shocked the first time a 14-year-old girl blamed me for not placing her with a relative.

I worked in a rural area and often felt isolated from coworkers because I had to drive so far to check on families. I began to look forward to getting home at night and having my favorite cocktail. My husband was a drinker too, and so dinner was often nonexistent or very late. We would sit and agree with each other about our world views and then fall asleep. While I was able to slow my drinking, he wasn't, and our marriage fell apart.

During my divorce, I felt like I was stressed to my breaking point. And I began to lose patience with my clients. I grew tired of the same parent excuses and the lack of attention from my supervisor. He was on "remote" as well—actually mostly on his farm immediately after work. He used to say there was no such thing as an emergency.

One day, I made a home visit and was really irritated when it was a school day and all the children answered the door in their pajamas. Their mom was a smoker, and the hot air and cigarette smoke hit me like a ton of bricks when I went inside. She answered my question about her children's school truancy by saying she just didn't think about it. I went ballistic! The entire family looked at me as though I had two heads. I left the house after my tirade, drove home, and proceeded to get drunk. To this day, no one knows.

My anger continued to grow, along with my sarcasm. Once I called the sheriff's department and complained to the chief without first speaking to the deputy who answered the phone in the first place. I was not in control. Nor was I doing good work. Eventually, I was required to see an employee assistance person. It wasn't something I did voluntarily, but it was a good thing to do. While I wasn't in love with my first therapist, enough was said for me to realize that I was pretty burned out. Therapy was not fast, like my insurance carrier wanted it to be. It took me a few years to unravel my childhood and rebuild my career.

I wish I knew then what I know now. Perhaps I could have avoided hurting people. Life is rough, and one of the things I had to actually learn was to take time to play as well as forgive myself for my mistakes. I am now a walking "burn-out prevention seminar."

Work-Related Symptoms

The good news is Clara worked through her burnout. Prior to that, however, she was a nasty event waiting to happen. Until she was forced by her boss to slow down, she was on a path to self-destruction.

Other work-related symptoms include misusing work breaks. We may have known a worker who started taking two-hour lunch breaks. Tardiness is another work-related burnout symptom. Remember the coworker who skidded into the parking lot late every morning because she overslept, got blindsided by another driver, or stood in line to pay for gas? There is the other colleague who spends more time at personal "appointments" than home visits. Burned-out workers will avoid being at work or will work almost to the point of obsession. The operative words here are "obsessive or avoidance behaviors." People who are burned out may also unconsciously draw attention to their problem by stealing or playing online games at work. On their way to burnout, some workers may feel righteous indignation with regard to lesser efforts made by more efficient coworkers.

Interpersonal Symptoms

Burnout can create exaggerated emotions and primitive or intellectualized communication. In Clara's case, she had increased her anger. Irritation usually affects emotional control and draws people into dangerous territory. One symptom is the inability to keep from crying. A worker has a problem if she forgets to stop crying in front of her clients.

Conversely, workers can withdraw from communication as well. Their writing can become cryptic or sarcastic, and their monosyllabic words may substitute for sentences. Conversely, another interpersonal burnout characteristic is hiding through intellectualism. People use big words to avoid clear communication. This is another way to distance themselves from feeling compassion while expressing anger in a passive-aggressive manner.

An inability to concentrate is a burnout symptom that absents workers mentally from staff or children and families. Workers can become so dis-

Am I Burned Out? A Checklist

Here are some burnout symptoms. If more than a few get checked, it may be a good idea to consider evaluating work habits and seeking help from family, coworkers, supervisors, a person of faith, or a therapist:

- I don't feel much of anything.
- I feel trapped in my job.
- My work overwhelms me.
- I cry more than I used to.
- I am a survivor of past trauma.
- I am startled quite easily.
- I feel helpless to change my work situation.
- I don't get much support from my supervisors.
- I feel distracted and have difficulty concentrating.
- I have frequent colds and infections.
- I use drugs or alcohol to take the edge off my anxiety.
- I feel angry most of the time.
- I am more irritable these days.
- I have difficulty sleeping, or I fall asleep easily but wake too early.
- I am beginning to feel numb about my clients.
- I dream a lot about work.
- My feelings get hurt more easily.
- I avoid doing work I do not enjoy.
- My chronic illness flares more often.
- I argue with people more often.
- I feel that I could use violence against child abusers.
- I feel isolated at work.
- I sleep too much.

- I dread going to work.

- I feel worthless.

- I am always tired.

- Sometimes, I place myself in needless danger.

- I do not feel as close to my clients as I used to.

- I work longer hours than most of my colleagues.

- I avoid work altogether.

- I feel anxious most of the time.

- I make more mistakes at work.

- The quality of my work has diminished.

- I have high standards, and I am extremely harsh with myself.

- I do not feel very confident.

- I feel detached from what is happening around me.

- I continue to feel dissatisfied even though I have changed jobs fairly often.

tracted that they find themselves walking into rooms and wondering why they are there. Lack of concentration can be more than a sign of old age.

How to Prevent Burnout

The best way to prevent burnout is to "know thyself." Identifying one's strengths and weaknesses is necessary. People can get into undesirable work situations and expect far too much of themselves if they do not know what they want.

Unfortunately, many people do not explore their internal selves until they are in crisis, but they can stop burnout if they begin to notice signs of slow burn. Some things people can do to prevent further decompensation are:

- Take vacation time even if you have nowhere to go.

- Make sure someone takes your calls when you are off the clock.

- Take a yoga or drawing class—something to disengage your brain.
- See a therapist.
- Find a mentor at work.
- Get new training.
- Form a peer supervision group.
- Talk to more experienced workers about how they cope with stress.
- List your stressors and see what you can prune from the list.
- Go to bed earlier.
- Exercise and cut out the heavy carbohydrates and caffeine.
- Say no to evening events.
- Turn off your cell phone and beeper.
- Delegate work at home and at work. Ask for help.
- Make time to do at least one relaxation activity a day.
- Write your goals for the next work day.
- Do not put off making decisions.
- Spend time outdoors.
- Get a massage.
- Surround yourself with supportive friends who are not all child welfare workers.

How to Deal with Burnout

Any painful condition like burnout provides an opportunity for growth, because crisis forces us to evaluate our old habits. Most people learn through suffering. It opens us to a more authentic state. But each crisis is terribly uncomfortable, and we can find ourselves in a state of anxiety.

Ironically, when people experience burnout, they tend to hang on more tightly to familiar habits. When the anxiety will not go away, however, they are forced to consider other choices. They may not know that burnout is a state of vulnerability. It puts them at a crossroads in their lives.

Feeling vulnerable can lead us to feel guilt-ridden and extremely self-critical. Taking excessive responsibility for all that happens to us is typical. Consequently, shame and embarrassment are predictable feelings. People naturally want to hide from the realization they are not perfect, but frailties become less powerful when one accepts them. Experiencing burnout is a wake-up call to discard unnecessary baggage.

Steps to Overcoming Burnout

The first thing to do if one chooses to work through burnout is to slow things down and become more aware of one's physical and emotional condition. The obvious solution is to take personal days, but if that is not possible, cancel personal appointments and get some rest.

The second step is to work at adopting patience with oneself and others. Getting to the burnout stage takes time, and physical and emotional healing is not immediate. Patience is a daily practice. Practicing breathing or slow exercise can help one become more observant and patient. Changing perspectives by literally changing scenery is helpful as well.

Next, workers need to examine old habits with compassion. One of the most difficult things for people to do is list 10 things they like about themselves. Workers reach burnout due to a number of reasons. Not all of them are the workers' fault, and burnout has nothing to do with being bad. Remember, all the saints we know are dead.

Along these lines, it is helpful to reassess one's expectations for oneself and others. Sometimes, all we can do is our best; even then, the situation may get worse. When workers examine expectations for clients, they can recognize that sometimes a little change is the best they can expect.

In overcoming burnout, workers need to practice new habits, but first, they need to know which ones to adopt. This is where self-awareness comes into play. What do we like to do? What makes us excited, eager, or curious? Old habits are hard to break, but it is easier when we are excited about adopting new ones.

When working through burnout, it is important to practice new behavior and thinking, because practicing them leads to confidence, and subsequently, success. For example, instead of saying, "When I make a mistake, I feel bad," practice thinking or saying aloud, "When I make a mistake, I learn." It takes time for brains to develop new sensitized neural pathways,

What Works Best for You?

Here is a list of questions intended to help you identify what works for you. Take time with it, and write down any personal awareness.

- How do I get along with my present boss?
- Do I prefer working alone or with others?
- What sort of organization do I enjoy working for?
- How often would I like to communicate with the person who supervises my work?
- Do I prefer to speak with someone or send a memo?
- Do I prefer written or oral communication?
- When do I have trouble communicating with people?
- Do I prefer short- or long-term projects?
- If I were in charge of my agency, what would I do?
- How do people respond when I am in charge?
- I need to have clear direction.
- I do not like close supervision.
- What are my biggest pressures?
- Why did I leave my last job?
- What would my boss say about my work performance?
- I (don't) enjoy repetitive tasks.
- I like details.
- What have I learned from my previous jobs?
- How do I handle being evaluated?
- How do I organize my daily activities?
- What type of person is difficult for me to work with?
- What is my favorite pastime?

- How do I define cooperation?

- How do I express my anger?

- What are the pros and cons about working in child welfare?

- I believe my work is an extenuation of my personal life.

- I get bored easily.

- I become more emotional about my pets then children on my caseload.

- What skills have I acquired at my job?

- How do I define doing a good job?

- How do I keep a positive attitude?

- What books have affected me the most?

- How do I take direction?

- How many projects can I handle at a time?

- How much money do I need to make?

- What am I looking for in my next job?

- How do I feel about my present caseload?

- How do I respond when people reject my ideas?

- I am more interested in a job than a career.

- How do I relax?

so repetition is the key to change. Few people learn a skill after a couple of tries. Change happens over time. Timelines in adopting new habits of thinking are more realistic when they are viewed in weeks and months.

Lastly, through the process of renewal, workers may be challenged to make brave decisions that will affect their lives. For example, they may need to speak up, take a stand, or simply consider other career opportunities. Taking responsibility for improving one's well-being is scary but absolutely necessary in overcoming burnout.

The Other Side of Burnout

The opposite of burnout is authentic appreciation for the opportunity to work with children and families. It is a state that allows workers to participate fully and leave the job behind at the end of the day. Most people will experience burnout during some point in their careers. It is not the end of the world. Yet how they acknowledge and work through their condition, while learning from their experience, has a lot to do with their resiliency in the future.

Ithaka

On your way back to Ithaka

Pray that the journey be long.

One discovery every night.

A long road with cyclops and monsters.

Laistrygonians and poseidon in rage.

Don't be afraid...

All you need to do to avoid them

Is raise your thoughts to the other space

Where your spirit and your body

Find sensation in the different and new.

No cyclops, no monsters,

No laistrygonians, no angry poseidon

On this road unless

You decide to bring them along

Pinned to the walls of your soul......

(Excerpted from a poem by Constantine Cavacy; translated by Antonio T. deNicolas)

References

Figley, C. R. (Ed.). (1995). *Compassion fatigue: Coping with secondary traumatic stress disorder in those who treat the traumatized.* Bristol, PA: Brunner/Mazel.

Kreisher, K. Burned out. (2002). *Children's Voice, 11*(4), 6–11.

Additional Resources

Alwon, F., & Reitz, A. (2000). *The workforce crisis in child welfare.* Washington, DC: CWLA Press.

Bartle, E. E., Couchonnal, G., Canda, E. R., & Staker, M. D. (2002, January). Empowerment as a dynamically developing concept for practice: Lessons learned from organizational ethnography. *Social Work: Journal of the National Association of Social Workers,* 39–40.

Beadle, A. D. (2002, March). Staff shortages abets attack on counselor. *Youth Today: The Newspaper on Youth Work,* p. 8.

Bischoff, R. J., Barton, M., Thober, J., & Hawley, R. (2002, July). Events and experiences impacting the development of clinical self confidence: A study of the first year of client contact. *Journal of Marital and Family Therapy,* 371.

Chodron, P. (2001). *The places that scare you: A guide to fearlessness in difficult times.* Boston: Shambahala.

Wendover, R. W. (2002). *Smart hiring: The complete guide to finding and hiring the best employees* (3rd ed.). Naperville, IL: Sourcebooks.

CHAPTER 9

The Resilient Child Welfare Worker

I Guess I Just Get Past My Difficulties

Pete's Story

Pete grew up in a New York City suburb. When he was only 5, his father was murdered, and the following year, both sets of grandparents died, leaving Pete's mother alone to raise two boys on a state hospital kitchen worker's salary. Pete laughs now when he thinks about how his mother communicated his father's death. "She said 'Your dad's on vacation,'" not, 'Your dad died,'" he comments.

A few years, later his mom married a man named Clay, who was a racist. Pete is Hispanic, and his stepfather was extremely cruel. "I remember watching Clay pass by in his car while my brother and I walked," remarks Pete. "He used to say to me, 'The darker you are, the dumber you come.'"

The family was poor, and Pete's clothes and eating utensils were initialed, "New York State." Entertainment was limited to occasional Chinese food and a movie on Friday nights.

Pete's teachers liked him, and he found his way into the hearts of the librarians who worked at the library down the road. Life was tough, but the boy's winning personality and good disposition helped him get through the years.

Sadly, as he grew into manhood, he became an alcoholic. He reports ritualizing his drinking by donning a top hat and visiting his father's former haunts. Yet he eventually made friends with people who were willing to help him stop drinking. He has celebrated his Alcoholic Anonymous anniversary every fourth of July for the last 30 years.

After becoming sober, Pete worked his way through college and graduate school. As years passed, he was promoted to top child welfare positions. Now he enjoys mentoring new workers and continues to inspire others when he shares his resiliency story through his seminars and books.

What Is Resilience?

Researchers have studied human resiliency for more than 50 years. It was popularized by a study conducted by Emmy Werner and Ruth Smith that tracked high-risk children in Hawaii for 35 years. *Human resilience* has been defined as the ability to overcome the obstacles from childhood, steer through adversities, bounce back from crisis, and reach out toward challenges (Reivich & Shatte, 2002).

A resilient child welfare worker may have been involved as a child with child welfare or experienced a somewhat traumatic childhood. A resilient worker could also be someone who learns from personal crisis and has no illusions that life is easy. A resilient child welfare worker often chooses to take on new work projects or lead coworkers. Pete is an excellent example of a resilient child welfare worker.

According to Dave Bundy, President of Children's Home Society of Florida, he notices resilient workers quickly. "They demonstrate optimism, determination, and a willingness to say what they need in order to get a job done." He described a woman in his agency who cheerfully takes on new assignments. He admires her upbeat personality and fearlessness.

Resilience Characteristics

Resilient individuals exhibit many of the following characteristics:

- **Use of natural intelligence and common sense.** A popular 1990s book, *Emotional Intelligence*, described the benefits of using both social and intellectual skills to successfully deal with life. Resilient workers are emotionally intelligent. They adopt the right character mask according to each situation, know how to assess a situation, and build a strategy most helpful to children and families. They are also creative in solving problems, such as finding the best way to compassionately tell a parent that his or her child will be temporarily placed in foster care.

- **Belief that what happens is for the best.** Resilient workers accept disappointments with equanimity. They often believe that they have more control at times than they actually do, but their belief gets them through rough patches.

- **Assessment of risk.** Resilient workers have the ability to forecast potential problems. They can anticipate risky situations and develop prevention plans. For example, a resilient worker may notice a change in a recovering parent's behavior. He or she develops two intervention alternatives. One plan includes going forward with child-parent reunification, but discussing relapse prevention. Another plan involves asking for an additional drug relapse evaluation from a court-appointed evaluator before placing the child back home.

- **Appreciation of the work experience.** Resilient people find meaning in their work, such as a mentor or coworker who role modeled love for child welfare work. These people feel that what they do is the most meaningful work in the world and feel blessed to help children and families.

- **Calm under pressure.** Resilient people often make great child welfare workers because they remain calm under pressure. Resilient workers usually have some control over their emotions during crisis. They have the ability to later put a healthy spin on the event, which helps them put it into perspective.

- **Understanding that events are temporary.** Whether because they have lived through tough circumstances or are intuitive, resilient people know that difficulties will pass and events are temporary. They do not expect life to be easy and may appear overly optimistic because they have a deeper understanding that life is change.

- **A sense of humor and play.** Resilient workers have a good sense of humor and do not take themselves too seriously. They usually make fun of their own mistakes and make others laugh. A good sense of humor goes a long way when working with difficult and confusing cases. Communicating a message through humor gets a lot further than expressing it through frustration or anger. Resilient workers can be like comedians who are able to introduce controversial topics while making people laugh. Resilient workers be found donning clown suits or playing soccer with their young clients. They like to play!

- **Knowing when to stop what they are doing.** Resilient child welfare workers have an internal gyroscope that gets them back on track. For example, Carol was the director of her county's children's services in Ohio. When she was asked why she decided to leave her job after many years of service, she responded, "I always believed that I would know when it was time to step down....I plan to stay in child welfare work and there are a number of things I can do. But I'm ready to move on." The ability to know when to leave is inherent in the resilient child welfare worker.

- **Centeredness.** Resilience researchers refer to this as "an inner locus of control." Resilient child welfare workers know who they are, in spite of the fact that others have tried to have them believe otherwise. In Pete's case, he never entertained the idea that he was not smart just because his stepfather said so. Resilient people will not be persuaded to go in a direction they know is wrong for them.

- **Expression of honest thoughts and feelings.** In the complex world of child welfare, it is always refreshing to meet people who do not beat around the bush. Chances are, the people who come to the point are resilient, because being honest and open is another resiliency characteristic trait.

- **Belief that child welfare work is spiritual.** "Spiritual beings engaged in a human experience rather than human beings engaged in a spiritual experience," is a phrase that applies to resilient workers. Resilient workers believe that work is an extension of their spiritual lives. This belief is expressed through a wide range of beliefs and practices.

- **Compassion.** The ability to feel compassion or empathy is an integral part of the resilient worker. Because of their capacity to relate to others with compassion, resilient people tend to feel less isolated. They can reach out more easily. Compassion compels them to do their best job and take on projects when there is a strong need.

- **Demonstration of adaptive distancing.** Resilient workers know when to get out of their own way. They understand the importance of setting boundaries and avoiding burnout. They do not become entangled in a dysfunctional office environment or overstep boundaries with clients. They maintain distance by leaving their work at the office.

- **Hope and optimism.** Resilient workers view their clients' situations as opportunities for growth. They can see crisis situations from a positive perspective and they project positive expectations toward their goals and objectives. They have the ability to anticipate a bright professional future and work to keep themselves from becoming bored.

- **Seeking out of mentors.** Most resilient people report that they were helped in their careers by a mentor. Resilient workers are open to being coached along their career path. Mentoring is an important part of learning resiliency, because a worker can avoid making mistakes with a teacher to guide him or her. In Pete's case, he had two or three mentors until he began to mentor others. His guidance came from a community college professor, and later, a Hispanic elder. Finally, he was encouraged by an older supervisor who continues to check Pete's work.

- **Giving meaning to their suffering.** Resilient child welfare workers are probably not happy to encounter tough situations, but they have the ability to recover from them and move ahead. For example, as a result of their personally devastating experiences, two women formed Mothers Against Drunk Driving in 1981. Today, there are more than 600 chapters throughout the United States. These women were able to give their suffering meaning. Many resilient child welfare workers chose their career because they suffered personal tragedy as well. Others rise to face incredible challenges as they work to manage reduced budgets, debilitating caseloads, and angry clients.

How Do I Become More Resilient?

Research has focused on people who seem naturally resilient, but plenty of others grow to be resilient because they have a sincere desire to enjoy their work. Here are some things you can do to become a resilient child welfare worker.

Examine Depression and Resilience

Information has substantiated the association between depression and pessimism, leading to a reduced capacity to bounce back from life's setbacks. Researchers have found that depressed people were accurate in assessing the pitfalls of any given situation, but resilient or optimistic people were not.

Furthermore, when depressed and nondepressed people were placed on panels together, the depressed group accurately judged themselves to be less socially attractive. Observers commented that the depressed group was not as persuasive or likable as their counterparts. And yet, the resilient group was judged to be somewhat grandiose because they believed they were even more likable than assessed by observers. In addition, depressed people were judged to have better memories about their failures. Consequently, research points to optimists' distorting their reality and pessimists' reporting reality more accurately (Seligman, 1992). The evidence does not suggest that optimists are liars or deceitful, it only reports that they probably get through their harsh experiences by giving them less negative meaning.

Pessimists are not wholly bad for any organization, but if their numbers are overabundant, the agency can lose sight of its vision and inertia can take over. Pessimism promotes depression and anxiety. Even when accurately projecting a mistake in the organization, pessimists do not feel any gratification. In transforming a pessimistic worker, it is best to put him or her with a more optimistic group.

Move Toward Optimism

A good way to evaluate for depression is to check with a mental health professional who has the capacity to make an assessment and refer to a psychiatrist qualified to determine if one would benefit from an antianxiety or antidepressant medication. Depression can also be linked to an imbalance in neurochemical orientation.

Exercise is one of the best antidotes to depression. The late Fred Rogers, creator of "Mr. Rogers Neighborhood," discussed his daily swim as his way to feel physically alert and optimistic.

Eating whole-grain foods and fresh vegetables is another depression fighter. Staying away from the wrong kind of carbohydrates helps beat depression. One child welfare worker called her friend for help six months after her husband's death. She was feeling suicidal. She had been eating a substantial amount of potato chips and soda since the funeral and not exercising. Her depression was severe and was increased by her food intake. Although her mood was not solely a result of her eating, her nutritional intake did not help.

Examine Beliefs About Trust and Personal Expectations

Linked with depression are habitual negative thoughts that form beliefs and world view. The majority of our beliefs are formed in childhood as sensitized neural pathways that can eventually affect our behavior.

Building resiliency also means reexamining what we tell ourselves when we are disappointed in others. We may swing from being overly cynical to

---

A Simple Exercise

To transform negative beliefs, one must build new neural pathways that become reinforced through practice. For example, to be a resilient thinker, a worker must consistently practice thinking about seeing life from a less negative perspective. Here is an easy exercise:

Fill in the blank:

- When I make a mistake, I tell myself I'm <u>what?</u>

- When I am disappointed, I tell myself I'm <u>what?</u>

- When I'm frightened, I tell myself I'm <u>what?</u>

- When I am sad, I tell myself I'm <u>what?</u>

   If you would prefer to tell yourself something different, what would it be for each of the above questions?

> *Practice each day by inserting your preferable comment into your thinking. You may slowly feel more optimistic. For example:*
>
> • When I make a mistake, I tell myself I'm <u>learning.</u>
>
> • When I'm disappointed, I tell myself <u>it's not always about me.</u>
>
> • When I'm frightened, I tell myself <u>what happened in the past is not happening now.</u>
>
> • When I'm sad, I tell myself <u>I will be okay.</u>

completely trusting. Some workers unconsciously look for people to disappoint them, further reinforcing their beliefs. People who have a hard time trusting may continue to have unrealistic expectations about people who are not capable of being trustworthy. When changing beliefs about trust, practice around people who are less likely to disappoint you.

Child welfare workers with trust issues may want to rethink their personal expectations if they are disappointed daily. The high expectations they place on others are usually reflective of the high expectations they place on themselves.

External factors that contribute to depression can affect thinking, too, because workers can internalize them by taking responsibility for the bad things that occur in their lives. Part of becoming more resilient is digesting the fact that a worker is not always responsible for someone else's behavior. Coworkers and even clients can project their feelings or frustrations onto others. One worker said:

> *I felt like the most miserable worker last week because I made a mistake in sharing too much information with a foster parent. Even when I apologized, she didn't back down. Her anger was so intense. It simply didn't match the crime. After a while, I was able to understand that if I take responsibility for doing something wrong, that's the best I can do.*

When people begin to practice preferable ways of thinking, they can find themselves caught between two internal voices. "Why waste my time?" is one voice. "This is and will be helpful," is another. When workers feel pulled back into negative thinking, they must ask, How does it help me to continue my old way of thinking? They can let go more easily when they are sure their old thinking is not personally helpful.

Build on Positive Experiences and Practice What Works

Why do we enjoy hearing upbeat music? Most people say that it lifts our spirits and energizes us. The same thing happens when we practice new behaviors and thinking. If we recognize that smiling affects our mood, why not smile? If we thoroughly explain the reasons why we made a placement decision and people respond with less emotion, why not explain? And if centering through prayer or meditation starts our day more calmly, why not practice prayer or meditation?

Taking risks by trying beneficial practices, such as a new hobby or sport, is part of building resilience. As we grow in confidence, we strengthen our optimism.

Set Manageable Goals

Build on positive new practices by setting short-term goals that help create confidence. Design manageable objectives when changing old behaviors and thinking. Try putting yourself on a realistic timeline to feel less depressed. When starting a new exercise program, begin slowly. When discussing a difficult topic with a supervisor, write your comments down and practice them over a few days. If a parent wants an immediate conversation and it is necessary but not time driven, schedule it for a time best suited to your biological clock. (For example, people have less energy right after lunch.)

We have more control over our success than we may think. Success brightens people's outlooks and initiates positive expectations for other activities.

Examine the Lives of Resilient People

The children's book, *The Little Engine That Could*, continues to be popular because it inspires children not to give up when the going gets tough. This metaphorical story is extremely powerful and continues to be remembered long after children become adults. The engine is a resiliency symbol.

Inspiring people are human symbols who help others become resilient child welfare workers. People often report that the person they most admire is a relative or other personal acquaintance. One child welfare worker glowingly spoke about his father, who always did his best even when he was given demeaning work.

Most of the famous people who inspire us did not realize they were role modeling when they were trying to accomplish their goals. They simply wanted to make things better for themselves or others. Often, they ran into extremely challenging circumstances, and many died poor or violently before their dreams were realized. Yet they inspire because they were resilient. They changed societies or created movements because they had the capacity to look beyond the current realities and follow a vision that in the end turned out well, sometimes long after they died.

To become more resilient, workers need inspiring people to be their examples for fighting back, moving forward, or taking risks. When we study their lives, we understand that they were human beings too, which makes it easier to follow their example.

Seek Out Mentors

Workers can learn from resilient mentors. For example, we can look past the anger from our clients if a mentor lets us know that dealing with angry people is part of the job. Here are some other examples:

> Susan was upset one day, when she found out her hours were changed. Her mentor let her know that every 12 weeks, she could expect to a shift change because that is how the administrator liked to work.

> Steve did not realize that he was supposed to follow up on a case until his mentor told him that although it was not mandatory, it was the best way to create a positive outcome for his client.

> Jen was not happy when she inherited a lot of work from a sick coworker. Her mentor said that if she took it on with a positive attitude, it would help her get the promotion she had been seeking.

Krista Goldstine-Cole learned invaluable lessons from her mentor. She taught high school students in a particularly racist area of her West Coast community. As a teacher, she chose to stand up to students and faculty members who leaned toward white supremacy and anti-Semitism. Her only support was the one older, African American instructor who "taught me not to be diverted from my goal by being distracted or bulldozed."

Eventually Krista moved on, but never forgot his immense character. She has become a mentor herself, especially when she shares this wisdom: "I think it's morally wrong to blame our children for societal problems if we don't stand up against them ourselves."

Practice Spirituality

The majority of workers surveyed for this book referred to their spirituality when they discussed what motivates them toward this work. *Webster's Ninth Collegiate Dictionary* (1990) defines spirituality "as the quality or state of relating to sacred matters." The word *spiritual* comes from the Latin word "spiriatus," meaning breathing or of wind (*Webster's*, 1990).

What is sacred to one person may not be sacred for another. Chris refers to walking in the woods as a sacred practice, whereas Tony is involved in capturing the spirit of Jesus when he attends church. Mohammed prays each morning. All these practices give people an opportunity to replenish their spirits.

Give Your Suffering Meaning

In Pete's story, he was able to use his childhood suffering to help children later. He understood how it felt to be stereotyped because of the way he looked. He knew that his alcoholism probably grew from depression and pain. He had empathy for the youth in residential placement and knew how to relate to their suffering.

In the book *Finding Meaning In Life*, Robert C. Leslie stated, "Every person is the most qualified expert in one field; his own life" (as cited in Fabry, Bulka, & Sahakian, 1979). Perhaps this means that people know the best way to transform their past suffering into a loftier endeavor. You may wish to think about learning from your former painful experiences. Creating a personal resilience story can help you. Here are some examples of how other child welfare workers gave their suffering meaning:

> *When Kasey was doing her social work internship, she did not feel very successful. She felt dumb because she had never worked with Asian clients. She did not understand what to do. In the process, she acted on some of her unsophisticated assumptions. Clients complained to her*

Create a Personal Resilience Story

Consider a mildly challenging experience. With the experience in mind, write a resilience story that includes how you would overcome it and give it meaning. Instead of using your real name, attach one of your favorite characters or animals to yourself. Then think of a helper who would deliver a healing message. Give that message bearer a fictitious identity as well. In the story, describe

- the challenge,

- how you are helped,

- what you do to overcome your experience, and

- how you put your experience to good use.

Begin your story by writing, "Once upon a time..." Give it a happy ending.

supervisor, and she was corrected. Kasey felt humiliated and deflated. She could have allowed the experience to permanently discourage her, but she set out to learn everything about cultural competence. Her new knowledge led to her changing work habits and ended her internship on a positive note.

Stan thought he knew what he was doing when he placed a child back at home. The little boy was killed three days later by a babysitter. The agency was in chaos, and Stan was strongly reprimanded, but not dismissed. Feeling ostracized, he methodically studied why he had placed the child back home and vowed that he would not put another child back home because of a court-ordered timeline again. Stan redeemed himself in the eyes of his coworkers when he initiated new agency guidelines.

Latoya was not one to say much to anyone. She was shy, but it didn't help when she had to appear in court and share her opinion with the judge. One day, she became tongue-tied when asked a question. The judge became

*angry and threatened her with contempt of court if she did
not change her "attitude." The experience was devastating
because Latoya felt completely misunderstood. Her shame
diminished after a few days when she decided to take
action. She began to write down her thoughts and practiced speaking them aloud to her cat, Eddie. As Eddie listened, Latoya's confidence grew. Next, she practiced with
a close friend and finally felt ready for court. Although her
first attempt was rough, she managed to share her opinion
in front of the same judge without slowing down or falling
apart. She felt especially gratified when he complimented
her on her new presentation style.*

Setting Our Sights on Becoming Resilient

Becoming resilient provides many benefits. The significant one may be that
our quality of life is substantially improved because we enlarge our capacity to appreciate what is set before us.

Building resilient behavior takes practice. It does not happen overnight.
We have to work hard if we want to change our old habits. Every day, we
are given opportunities to realize that our lives have meaning by how they
are lived. We can begin now to build on positive thinking. After all, what
do we have to lose?

References

Fabry, J. B., Bulka, R. P., Sahakian, W. S. (Eds.). (1979). *Finding meaning in life:
Logotherapy.* Northvale, NJ: Jason Aronson.

Reivich, K., & Shatte, A. (2002). *The resilience factor: 7 essential skills for overcoming life's inevitable obstacles.* New York: Random House.

Seligman, M. E. P. (1992). *Learned optimism.* New York: Pocket Books.

Webster's ninth collegiate dictionary. (1990). Washington, DC: Merriam-Webster.

Additional Resources

Brohl, K. (1996). *Working with traumatized children: A handbook for healing.*
Washington, DC: CWLA Press.

Terez, T. (2002). *22 keys to creating a meaningful workplace*. Avon, MA: Adams Media.

Wendover, R. W. (2002). *Smart hiring: The complete guide to finding and hiring the best employees* (3rd ed.). Naperville, IL: Sourcebooks.

CHAPTER 10

A Call to Service

I Can't Imagine Doing Anything Else

Never put off until tomorrow what you can do today,
because if you enjoy it today, you can do it again tomorrow.

—*Anonymous*

This book has drawn a picture of 21st-century child welfare work by providing an overview of child welfare conditions and strategies about moving more effectively through its system. Yet this writing would not be complete without discussing why people are motivated to enter the field. The call to service is a remarkable human trait and largely inherent within child welfare workers.

Reasons and Service Vary

People work in child welfare for a variety of reasons and demonstrate their commitment to service in many ways. One foster mom mentioned that she was involved because service was just part of her character. Indeed, internal drive toward doing service is a chief motivator.

Many people become child welfare workers because of the satisfaction they feel. Others are driven by a moral purpose. Some workers adopt something called "stoic endurance" in their approach to working with kids. They may suffer financial or social deprivation to raise a grandchild or start an adoption agency because they want to see children be successful.

Others use their jobs to boost themselves to higher levels of management, giving their natural ambition meaning. Some workers simply enjoy learning and growing through their work. Some people feel personally affirmed or validated because their work brings them higher visibility and an opportunity to be recognized as helpers.

People demonstrate their call to service in different ways. They become engaged in child welfare work as volunteers and paid professionals. Volunteer parents are doing child advocacy when they work in schools and youth or homeless shelters. Religiously sanctioned workers work in behalf of children as missionaries or church delegates. They may work at day care centers or afterschool programs in parts of the country with great need.

Nonprofit agency workers at mental health or drug and alcohol centers advocate at several levels to intervene and support children. National child welfare associations' staffs lobby hard to pass proactive legislation.

Administrators at foundations, such as the Annie E. Casey Foundation, underwrite children's projects and vigorously advocate for innovative interventions. Community volunteers may restore homes or share their earnings to provide clothes, toys, food, and holiday cheer. Government workers in child protection agencies, foster care, schools, courts, and law enforcement strive to ensure that child safety is ensured.

Finally, neighbors and friends often become natural child welfare helpers when they look out for children and caregivers by sharing their friendship or partnering with a larger entity such as neighborhood watch. Mad Dads, a national organization with a mission to promote responsible fathering, speaks out against drugs or violence and is an example of a natural helper group.

For every grand project promoted by child welfare leaders, thousands of small yet significant ones are brought about because of child welfare advocates working on the front lines. Every day, child welfare workers make a difference. "A good deal of talent is lost in this world for want of a little courage," wrote one author. Yet courage is not lacking in most child welfare workers. Reggie, a child welfare worker, supports this truth when he said, "If I see a fire reported on the evening news, I jump into my car to make sure my clients are unharmed." He is just one of the thousands of workers who look past their own safety to help kids.

Surveys Reflect Worker Commitment

This book has made reference to more than 100 surveys completed by child welfare workers in the United States. Their responses often mentioned challenges specific to their region or work specialty. But they were in agreement when they answered one question: "Why do you continue to be a child advocate?" Their universal response was that they were committed to helping kids. This is a small sample of their answers, and they reveal a shared attitude about their work:

> Larry from Arizona remarked that he really couldn't retire. "The work keeps me engaged and draws me back to the needs of the children."

> Krista from Washington State said, when asked what she liked best about her work, "It's a great opportunity to do good." She added, "The kids need us!"

> Marie from Florida said that she "liked making a difference" and wanted to "provide love and support."

> Ana from Washington, D.C., said, "I love to help families by respecting their culture and values." She too wanted to make a difference in people's lives because they made a difference in hers.

> Maureen stated that the thing she liked best were "hugs and smiles from the children." She also said that child welfare work was "a calling since [she was] a teen."

> Samantha said that what she liked most about her work was "that I am there for all of my kids and that sometimes my involvement is what they need and I make a difference." She went on rather elegantly to say: "I continue to be a child advocate because I am still learning a lot about what I might be able to accomplish in terms of providing more necessary and specific services. But mostly, although it sounds like a cliché, I continue because I believe children are the future and I feel so many kids are missing out on so much in life. If I can open a door, any door to a different reality, to one kid, then it is worth the effort I put in with all of them."

Denise stated, "I love working with kids and their parents and I believe in them. I accept them for who they are."

Larry from Chicago wrote that the work was "rewarding, and I do see progress."

Paree wrote that she continues to be a child advocate because, "It's not superficial! People are fascinating. There's joy in helping others. There is always more to learn."

Mark wrote that "I am doing God's work," and it is "my life mission."

Regina continues in child welfare work because, "Someone is still asking for help."

Tershea likes "seeing families succeed." She believes her work to be "fulfilling."

Deborah C. said that she likes "when a family takes advantage of support services and the kids gain from that." Deborah also stated, "I care about the welfare of children. I believe they deserve every chance we have to help them to succeed."

Alda liked most about her work, "Empowering families to advocate for themselves. I care about children and families who are at risk and in need of services."

Melissa wrote simply, "Children are wonderful!"

From New England, Chris said that, "I can impact on a multigenerational level and see opportunities and results at family services."

One worker said, "I strive to make a difference, no matter how big or small!"

Barbara stated that, "I believe I can plant seeds of hope and I have seen change and progress."

Vera P. likes "being able to work on young people's behalf, directly with children" and "giving back to the members of the inner city community."

Paul H. says that "I believe a lot of our young people are being mistreated in this society and I want to help them."

Allison continues in child welfare work because, "Children are our future and because they have a lot to say and have much insight at times."

And finally, Glenn M. said quite precisely that he stays in the work because, "Children, adolescents, and young adults count!"

Although child welfare workers are not pleased with many of their work conditions, they are clear about feeling satisfaction in helping children and youth. Intervening to save a young life, teaching new skills to a teenager, or guiding caregivers toward personal transformation gives them purpose.

As child welfare workers, we must never minimize what we do by bowing to our culture's tendency to covet jobs that bypass human service. Experiencing contentment usually happens when we give meaning to our lives. Our work is unique because it provides us with countless opportunities to realize true satisfaction.

In this new century, dedicated child welfare workers are exploring uncharted territory. Technical, cultural, and social norms are rapidly changing. It is providing us with Herculean challenges. Overcoming them is daunting, but necessary. We are the new miracle workers!

Additional Resources

Coles, R. (1993). *The call of service.* New York: Houghton Mifflin.

Frankel, V. E. (1979). Foreword. In J. B. Fabry, R. P. Bulka, & W. S. Sahakian (Eds.), *Finding meaning in life: Logotherapy.* Northvale, NJ: Jason Aronson.

Jones, R., & Welch, L. (2003, February 2). The guardian. *New York Times Magazine,* 86.

Terez, T. (2002). *22 keys to creating a meaningful workplace.* Avon, MA: Adams Media.

About the Author

Kathryn Brohl, MA, a Licensed Marriage and Family Therapist, has worked in child welfare for more than 30 years. She is the author of four other books and coeditor of one. Brohl has written and produced child welfare–oriented videos and trains child welfare workers throughout the United States, Canada, and Australia. She has also cohosted a nationally syndicated radio program. She lives in Jacksonville, Florida, with her husband, Phil.